Richard Wagner
Siegfried

Richard Wagner
Siegfried

translation and commentary
by Rudolph Sabor

**For Emilie, Samuel
and Rosemarie**

Phaidon Press Limited
Regent's Wharf
All Saints Street
London N1 9PA

First published 1997
© 1997 Phaidon Press Limited

ISBN 0 7148 3653 2

A CIP catalogue record for this
book is available from the
British Library

Printed in Hong Kong

Frontispiece, Bernd Aldenhoff
as Siegfried in the Bayreuth
production of 1951

Contents

Foreword

There is an overriding need for a new translation of Wagner's libretto to *Der Ring des Nibelungen*: the section entitled 'Translating Wagner's Ring' explains why and also specifies the particular aims of this author's version; for further discussion on the vital topic of the German *Idiom* and the individual language assigned by Wagner to each of his characters, the reader is directed to the companion volume of this series.

The main section of this volume – and of the three that cover respectively *Das Rheingold*, *Die Walküre* and *Götterdämmerung* – consists of the German text of the *Ring*, which runs side by side with its English translation. Each leitmotif, as it appears, is indicated in the margin, which also carries the author's annotations on points of particular musical or textual interest. The occurrence of each leitmotif is given beside the German text, its first appearance in bold print. The syllable on which a leitmotif begins is shown by italic print (where no syllable is italicized, the motif begins after the line of text). Leitmotifs sounding sequentially are listed from left to right. (In naming the leitmotifs the author has adopted Hans von Wolzogen's nomenclature where it was found to be helpful, but has substituted his own terminology wherever necessary.) A synopsis of the plot and step-by-step breakdown of the action begin each act. The leitmotifs new to the act are identified with musical quotations, and there is a brief discussion of the motifs' musical and dramatic character.

As well as providing a new translation of Wagner's libretto for *Siegfried*, this volume discusses the crucial problem facing Mime in Act I, how to teach Siegfried fear. In 1857 Wagner interrupted his work on Act II, to complete the opera almost fourteen years later; reasons for this are given in 'Siegfried Abandoned!'. Appendices include details of *Siegfried's* composition and performance, a selective bibliography and discography, and a videography; the volume concludes with a comprehensive list of all leitmotifs that are heard in *Siegfried*.

A number of people have helped me in a number of ways. Hilde Pearton, Dr Maurice Pearton and Stewart Spencer have provided comments in detail and depth. Their generous assistance far exceeds the accepted norm of collegial co-operation, and I hope the present volumes reflect their good counsel. Eric Adler has supplied valuable information about *Ring* performances in distant climes. The unquenchable thirst for Wagnerian enquiry and intelligence displayed by the students of my seminars on Wagner at Crayford Manor and Higham Hall has been largely responsible for the growth and scope of these five volumes. Several enlightening conversations with Wolfgang Wagner, wise guardian of the Bayreuther Festspiele, have claimed the author's attention and have contributed to smoothing his path through the complexities of the *Ring*.

Emmi Sabor has double-checked the manuscript, and I am grateful for her labour and for the serenity with which she has tolerated Richard Wagner as lodger for the best part of our lives. Lady Young, with Wagnerian seductiveness, was instrumental in persuading Phaidon Press to publish a series of books whose structural and typographical intricacies were formidable. To my editors, Edmund Forey and Ingalo Thomson, and to Hans Dieter Reichert of hdr design, I owe particular thanks for their masterminding of our joint Wagnerian safari.

Rudolph Sabor, Petts Wood, 1997

Leitmotifs: an Introduction

Appreciating the power of Wagner's system of leitmotifs adds a new dimension to our understanding of the *Ring* cycle. There are those who maintain that a leitmotif is little more than a musical visiting card that announces a character's appearance or a dramatic event. This is a fallacy. The Wagnerian leitmotif is an integral element of the *Gesamtkunstwerk*, the totality of the arts – the union of music, poetry and stage craft. It comments on the action, it recalls, it predicts, it even contradicts, occasionally, a character's words or action, but it is always *bona fide*. Leitmotifs are our accredited guides through the profundities of the *Ring*.

To alert the listener to a new leitmotif's first appearance, Wagner generally repeats it, sometimes more than once, and he frequently prescribes an appropriate action to accompany the motif. A leitmotif undergoes many modifications in the course of the *Ring*. It may be varied melodically, rhythmically or harmonically, it may be played by instruments other than those which sounded it at its first appearance. Such modifications are generally inaugurated by either musical or psychological requirements.

Wieland Wagner (1917–66), the composer's grandson, pointed out that leitmotifs were symbols, and that tracing the course of such musical symbols through the entire *Ring* would amount to a journey of discovery into the realms of depth psychology. Such a course is traced in the companion volume of this series, in the essay 'The Wagnerian Leitmotif'.

The present volumes are committed to defining and interpreting the whole set of motifs, both separately and in the context of the drama, with the aim of equipping the reader with a genuine grasp of the complexities of the work.

Translating Wagner's *Ring*

Mimi hight a manikin grim,
who in nought but greed granted me care,
to count on me, when manful I'd waxed,
in the wood to slay a worm,
which long had hidden there a hoard.

More than a hundred years ago the English-speaking world was treated to a translation of the *Ring* by Frederick and Henrietta Corder, husband and wife; the above is a sample of their craft. The Corders had many successors. The most noteworthy are Frederick Jameson in 1896, Margaret Armour in 1911, Ernest Newman in 1912, Stewart Robb in 1960, William Mann in 1964, Peggie Cochrane in 1965, Lionel Salter in 1966, Andrew Porter in 1976 and Stewart Spencer in 1993.

Their translations have much to offer. I have admired and envied many of their neat solutions to intricate problems, and I am indebted to them all for suggesting a phrase here, a telling word there, and for the comfortable assurance of being a successor rather than a pioneer.

So why attempt a new translation? Because Wagner's *Ring*, in spite of minor flaws, is a literary masterpiece, something that none of the existing translations quite manages to convey. But the *Ring* is not only a literary work of art. Its intricate system of metrical patterns, its use of alliteration, its rare but telling rhymes, its imaginative metaphors, its occasional punning, its astonishing ambiguities, its sheer singability – all these combine to create something unique in the history of the opera libretto: the music is in the text. The present translation aims to provide the reader and singer with a libretto which does not sound like a translation, but rather like the text Wagner might have written had he been born not in Leipzig but in London. My objectives are:
– Accuracy
– Matching German and English lines, retaining the position of key words
– Preserving the original metre
– Retaining alliteration and rhyme where possible
– Elucidating where Wagner is obscure
– Emulating the original by allowing each character to speak in his/her particular idiom

Accuracy
Confusion can arise not only from grammatical errors in translation, but also from misunderstood figures of speech; mistranslation can obscure an already complex plot.

Matching Lines and Key Words
To assist the reader, it is essential that the German text and English translation run in parallel; lines must not be transposed just to satisfy grammatical demands. Equally important is the location of key words. Where the German speaks for example of 'Schwert' (sword) or 'Liebe' (love), the word may have been given a particular melodic or instrumental setting, which would be lost if the word were displaced in translation.

Metre
It has earlier been asserted that Wagner's music is already discernible in the text. This is achieved, partly, by the astonishing variety of metre: iambs (.-), trochees (-.), anapests (..-) and spondees (--), long lines and short lines. All coexist without ever disturbing the natural flow of the text.

Alliteration and Rhyme
Wagner regarded alliteration as the textual equivalent of the musical leitmotif. In three of his prose works, *Das Kunstwerk der Zukunft*, *Eine Mitteilung an meine Freunde* and *Oper und Drama*, he stresses the importance of that method of versification which is 'another kind of rhyme'. Indeed, the German term *Stabreim* means 'spelling rhyme'. The counterpart of the *Stabreim* is the true rhyme, which Wagner uses most sparingly in the *Ring*; when he does, it heralds a matter of special importance.

Obscurity and Ambiguity
On the few occasions when Wagner's language is convoluted and the meaning becomes opaque, the translator must lend a helping hand. Wagner's libretto can also include deliberate ambiguity, which must be preserved in the translation.

Characterization
The most important aspect of Wagner's versification is the individual idiom of his characters. Wagner's characterization does not begin on the stage: it is already planned in the language of the text, where each character is given his or her own distinctive mode of expression. It is up to the translator to retrace Wagner's design.

'Poetry is what gets lost in translation,' someone once said. It is the author's sincere wish that this may not be so.

The Story So Far

In *Rheingold* Alberich, lord of the subterranean Nibelungs, for-swears love. This enables him to steal the Rhinegold from its careless guardians, the Rhinemaidens. From the gold Alberich forges a ring which makes him, so he thinks, master of the world.

The giants Fafner and his brother Fasolt have built a fortress, 'Walhall', for Wotan and his fellow gods. Wotan has promised them as reward Freia, goddess of youth (relying on the cun-ning of Loge, god of fire, to save her); the giants, hearing about the magic ring fashioned from the gold, wish instead to be rewarded with the gold. They take Freia hostage until Wotan pays the new price.

Loge accompanies Wotan to Nibelheim, Alberich's domain, where Mime (Alberich's brother) has fashioned a magic helmet, the Tarnhelm; Alberich is captured by Wotan and Loge and has to buy his freedom with his gold, the Tarnhelm and the ring. Alberich puts a curse on the ring and all its future owners.

Wotan offers the gold to the giants as ransom for Freia. But they also demand the Tarnhelm and the ring. Wotan refuses to give them the ring, but Erda, the earth goddess, warns Wotan to yield, adding that the end of the gods is approaching. Wotan obeys, and Fafner kills Fasolt over possession of the ring (the curse is at work!).

The gods, led by Wotan, hail the illusory dawn of their power and security, and climb a rainbow bridge which leads to Wal-hall. Loge foresees the gods' demise and decides not to follow them.

Events between *Das Rheingold* and *Die Walküre*

1. Fafner has turned himself into a dragon, sleeping upon his golden hoard.

2. Travelling to the depths, Wotan has fathered Brünnhilde, his warrior maiden, with Erda.

3. Wotan has fathered another eight daughters, the Valkyries (Walküren), with an unnamed woman, possibly Erda.

4. On a journey to earth, Wotan, with a mortal woman, has fathered the twins Siegmund and Sieglinde.

Events of *Die Walküre*

Siegmund, pursued by enemies, seeks refuge in Hunding's forest hut. Sieglinde, Hunding's wife, revives the fugitive. She and Siegmund are attracted to each other. Hunding recognizes in Siegmund a deadly enemy; he offers him shelter for the night, but threatens to kill him the next day. When Hunding retires, Sieglinde shows Siegmund the sword in the tree trunk which had been lodged there by an old man (Wotan). Siegmund withdraws the sword and, realizing that they are brother and sister, the twin lovers escape. Wotan orders Brünnhilde to aid Siegmund in his battle with Hunding, but Fricka, guardian of wedlock, demands Siegmund's death. Brünnhilde disobeys and causes Wotan to play a part in the slaying of Siegmund. Brünnhilde rides away with Sieglinde. She tells her that she will give birth to Siegfried, greatest of heroes, and hands her the splinters of Siegmund's sword. Wotan punishes his disobedient daughter by locking her, defenceless, in slumber on a rocky mountain. Yielding to her pleas, Wotan surrounds the rock with a circle of flames which only a fearless hero may penetrate.

Events between *Die Walküre* and *Siegfried*

1. Since Siegfried's birth some eighteen years must be assumed to have elapsed.

2. Sieglinde has died giving birth to Siegfried. The splinters of Siegmund's sword have come into Mime's possession.

3. Mime has brought up Siegfried; he expects him to obtain the Nibelung hoard, which the lad will surely yield to his foster-father.

Characters of *Siegfried*

SIEGFRIED

Son of Siegmund and Sieglinde. Devised by Wotan as fearless hero who is to restore the gods' fortune. Reared by Mime, reforges his father's splintered sword, kills the dragon (Fafner), gains ring and Tarnhelm (magic cap), kills Mime, vanquishes an unknown 'guardian of the rock' (Wotan as Wanderer), penetrates the circle of flames, kisses Brünnhilde awake and weds her. Will be killed by Hagen, in *Götterdämmerung*. Tenor, in *Siegfried* and *Götterdämmerung*.

MIME

Nibelung, brother of Alberich, master smith. Rears the young Siegfried, in order to obtain the Nibelung hoard. Makes Siegfried confront and kill the dragon (Fafner). Fails in his attempt to poison Siegfried, who kills him. Tenor, in *Rheingold* and *Siegfried*.

WANDERER

Wotan, ruler of the gods, roams the world as observer. Challenges Mime to battle of wits, spares the loser's life, prophesies Mime's death at the hands of a fearless hero (Siegfried), tries to impede Siegfried's quest for Brünnhilde, in order to prove the hero's intrepidity. Has his spear shattered by Siegfried and relinquishes his rule. Bass-baritone, in *Rheingold, Walküre* and, as Wanderer, in *Siegfried*.

ALBERICH

Father of Hagen, brother of Mime. Ruler of the Nibelungs, dwarfs living in subterranean Nibelheim. Has renounced love and forged an all-powerful ring from the stolen Rhinegold. Loses his ring to Wotan, then curses it and all future owners. Intends to regain the ring and become ruler of the world. Fails to persuade the dragon (Fafner) to part with it, disputes eventual ownership with Mime, and rejoices over his brother's death. Baritone, in *Rheingold, Siegfried* and *Götterdämmerung*.

FAFNER

Giant, brother of Fasolt, kills him over possession of the cursed ring. Turns himself into a dragon and guards the Nibelung hoard. Is killed by Siegfried, but manages to warn him to beware of Mime. Bass, in *Rheingold*, and, as Dragon, in *Siegfried*.

ERDA

Earth-goddess, mother of the three Norns and of Brünnhilde. Represents knowledge of past and future. Deplores Wotan's punishment of Brünnhilde and declines to advise Wotan on restoring the gods' prosperity. Alto, in *Rheingold* and *Siegfried*.

WOODBIRD

Warns Siegfried to beware of Mime, advises him to obtain Fafner's ring and Tarnhelm, and shows him the way to Brünnhilde's rock. Soprano, in *Siegfried*.

BRÜNNHILDE

Valkyrie, daughter of Wotan and Erda. Had been punished by Wotan for aiding Siegmund in his battle with Hunding. Lies asleep on a rock, surrounded by a guardian fire. Becomes the bride of Siegfried, who penetrates the flames and kisses her awake. Soprano, in *Walküre*, *Siegfried* and *Götterdämmerung*.

Ernst Kraus as Siegfried and
Hans Breuer as Mime in a
Bayreuth production of the
early 1900s

Act I

Synopsis
Leitmotifs
Libretto

Act I: Story

A Forest Cave

Scene 1

Mime has set up his forge in the forest where Fafner, in the shape of a dragon, sleeps upon his hoard. Siegfried demands a sword from Mime, but the smith is unable to produce a weapon which the strong young lad cannot break into bits. The impatient Siegfried obtains information from his foster-father about his parents and about the fragments of his father's shattered sword. He orders Mime to reforge the sword and storms away.

Scene 2

Wotan, the Wanderer, enters and invites Mime to stake his head in a trial of knowledge. Each is to ask three questions of the other. Mime is unable to answer the Wanderer's final question, 'Who is to forge the fragments of the shattered sword?' The Wanderer supplies the answer himself: 'He who knows no fear shall forge the sword. As for your head, I leave it to him who has never learnt what fear is.' Left alone, Mime is in a state of terror. He will lose his head to Siegfried unless he can teach him fear. But if Siegfried learns fear, nobody will forge the sword which could kill Fafner, thus depriving Mime of the longed-for hoard.

Scene 3

Siegfried returns and asks for his sword, but Mime is anxious to teach him fear. He is unsuccessful, and Siegfried proceeds to melt down the splintered fragments and reforge his father's sword; Mime concocts a poisonous brew which he intends to offer Siegfried, as soon as the lad has killed the dragon.

Mime and the Wanderer;
illustration by Arthur Rackham
(1911)

Act I: Action

1. Orchestra: Prelude
2. Mime cannot forge the sword
3. Siegfried bullies Mime
4. Mime's complaint
5. Parentage discussion
6. The sword
7. Mime alone
8. The Wanderer answers three questions
9. Mime answers two questions
10. The Wanderer answers for Mime
11. Mime alone
12. Mime tries to teach Siegfried fear
13. Siegfried forges Nothung

Mime's hut; set design by
Joseph Hoffman, Bayreuth 1876

Act I: Leitmotifs

The leitmotifs new to the act follow in chronological order, together with the page number of first appearance.

Brooding p.24

Horn Call p.26

Adventure p.28

Crocodile p.30

MIME

Als zul-len-des Kind zog ich dich auf,

Longing p.34

Freedom p.46

SIEGFRIED

Aus dem Wald fort in die Welt ziehn: nim-mer kehr ich zu-ruck'

Wanderer p.48

Authority p.56

Shuffle p.58

Action p.78

Commentary on the Leitmotifs

Brooding

Two bassoons, a third apart, play this descending seventh, above a *pianissimo* timpani trill; the sound is veiled and mysterious. A warning to the listener – watch the perpetrator of those ghoulish growls.

Horn Call

Always associated with Siegfried, the Horn Call motif appears together with the young hero. Though initially announced by the strings, it is usually played by a boisterous French horn. Lavignac, an early commentator, named it, laboriously, 'Call of the Son of the Woods'.

Adventure

A hot-blooded motif, designed to portray the rebellious young Siegfried. In his autobiography, *Mein Leben*, Wagner recounts how the motif came to him:

'A tinker had established himself opposite our house, and stunned my ears all day long with his incessant hammering. In my disgust at never being able to find a detached house protected from every kind of noise, I was on the point of deciding to give up composing altogether until the time when this indispensable condition should be fulfilled. But it was precisely my rage over the tinker that, in a moment of agitation, gave me the theme for Siegfried's furious outburst against the bungling Mime. I played over the childishly quarrelsome 'racket' theme in G minor to my sister, furiously singing the words at the same time, which made us all laugh so much that I decided to make one more effort.'

Crocodile

The 'sobbing' embellishment on the second note is symptomatic of this oily, slippery, tear-jerking motif. Mime does not sing it, he sobs it – a perfect aural equivalent to the tears of the man-eating reptile.

Longing

This chromatically rising motif, played by the cellos and so evocative of *Tristan*, makes only a few appearances in *Siegfried*. Wagner directed his orchestra to play it 'as if emerging from a dream, coming from very far away'.

Freedom

A jaunty, folksong-like tune, with a second section that is closely related to Mime's 'Crocodile' song. The latter is in the minor key, acciaccatura-ridden and bogus, the former is in the major key, guileless and forthright. Freedom from entanglement is Siegfried's motto. In *Götterdämmerung* he will even leave his beloved Brünnhilde to the *Freedom* motif.

Wanderer

Horns and tubas proclaim this chromatic motif, which wanders from key to key. Its veiled tones are reminiscent of the Tarnhelm (*Rheingold*) and Oblivion (*Walküre*) motifs. Erich Rappl, a modern commentator, calls it 'Globetrotter' – ingenious, though somewhat latter-day.

Authority

This powerful motif symbolizes the power of Wotan. It clearly derives from the Genesis and Erda motifs. In *Götterdämmerung* it will be associated with the World Ash Tree from which Wotan obtained his spear and, with it, his authority.

Shuffle

Violas descend in slightly chromatic, slightly syncopated triplets, accompanying and representing Mime's uneasy, shambling demeanour.

Action

Cellos and double basses announce the Action motif as it accompanies Siegfried's mighty labour with the bellows and the pulverized sword (the lower voice of the motif). Later, to 'The cinders burn so bravely now', Siegfried sings a rhythmical variation of the upper part of the same motif. In both forms, the Action motif derives, quite logically, from Siegfried's earlier Freedom motif.

For an introduction to the leitmotifs in *Siegfried* that first appeared in *Das Rheingold and Die Walküre*, the reader should consult the author's translations of these works.

Siegfried: 'Forge me, my
hammer, a trusty sword!';
illustration by Norman Price

I. Akt: I. Szene

Wald

MIME
Zwangvolle Plage!
Forge   *Grief*   Müh ohne Zweck!
Das beste Schwert,
das je ich geschweisst,
in der Riesen Fäusten
hielte es fest:
doch dem ich's geschmiedet,
der schmähliche Knabe,
er knickt und schmeisst es entzwei,
Brooding   als schüf ich Kindergeschmeid!
Sword

Es gibt ein Schwert,
Sword   das er nicht zerschwänge;
Nothungs Trümmer
Forge   zertrotzt' er mir nicht,
könnt ich die starken
Stücken schweissen,
die meine Kunst
nicht zu kitten weiss!
Könnt ich's dem Kühnen schmieden,
meiner Schmach erlangt' ich da
Brooding   *Dragon*   Lohn!

Fafner, der wilde Wurm,
lagert im finstren Wald;
mit des furchtbaren Leibes
      Wucht
der Niblungen Hort
Sword   *Dragon*   hütet er dort.
Siegfrieds kindischer Kraft
Sword   *Ring*   er*läge* wohl Fafners Leib;

Act I: Scene 1

Forest

[A rocky cave with a smith's forge, large bellows, an anvil and other blacksmith's tools. Mime is hammering, with growing despondency, at a sword. He stops.]

MIME
Wearisome trouble!
Toil without end!
The finest sword
that ever I forged, –
if a giant gripped it,
it would not snap;
but he it was made for,
that insolent infant,
in splinters he shivers the sword,
as though I made him a toy!
[he throws the sword on the anvil and muses]
One sword I know
that he could not shatter:
Nothung's fragments
would baffle the boy,
could I but forge
the mighty metal,
which all my skill
cannot match or patch.
Were I to weld that weapon,
it would make amends for my
    shame.
[he sinks back, deep in thought]
Fafner, the dragon beast,
lurks in his bosky lair,
where the monster's mountainous
    bulk
on Nibelung gold
slouches and sleeps.
Siegfried, youthful and strong,
would soon cut short Fafner's life,

Accompanied by a long *pianissimo* roll on the timpani, two bassoons intone the Brooding motif. This is soon followed by the contrabass tuba's Treasure motif. The Forge motif is announced by gruff violas with a very quiet staccato in their lower ranges, while the bassoons now intone a whole series of Grief motifs. As the insistent Forge motifs grow louder, Ring motifs are heard, first on the clarinets, then on cor anglais, bassoons and oboes. Suddenly, a bass trumpet proclaims, *pianissimo*, the Sword motif, answered by Forge and Grief (low strings), before the curtain rises.

Both Mime and his brother Alberich seek the ring and the golden treasure which is in Fafner's possession. The giant has turned himself into a dragon, sleeping on his hoard. Mime plots his destruction: Siegfried is to kill the dragon with the newly forged sword, Nothung. But Mime also knows that forging the sword is beyond him: what was bequeathed by a god and was shattered by a god can be restored only by the god or his deputy. The music makes the point by simultaneously proclaiming the motifs of the Sword and Walhall, the latter being part of the Arrogance motif.

Through the motifs, the music tells us: Mime *Broods* how to obtain *Treasure* and *Ring*, while *Grieving* over his failure to *Forge* the appropriate *Sword*.

When the *Ring* was performed at Her Majesty's Theatre, London, in 1882, a critic wrote: 'Mime, a smith by trade, sets up his forge in a lonely wood, far from the busy haunts of men. The only other settler in the neighbourhood is a dragon. In such a situation Mime's chances of obtaining customers are obviously nil.'

In his poem (libretto) *Der junge Siegfried* Wagner presents Mime as 'short, malformed, his head disproportionately large, piercing, red-rimmed eyes, shaggy beard, bald head'. He warned the singer not to play for laughs: 'Mime is thoroughly sinister.'

des Niblungen Ring
erränge er mir.

Sword Nur ein Schwert taugt zu *der* Tat;
nur Nothung nützt meinem Neid,
Sword wenn Siegfried sehrend *ihn*
Arrogance schwingt:
und ich kann's nicht schweissen,
Forge Nothung, das *Schwert*!

Zwangvolle Plage!
Müh ohne Zweck!
Das beste Schwert,
das je ich geschweisst,
nie taugt es je
zu der einzigen Tat!
Ich tappre und hämmre nur,
weil der Knabe es heischt:
er knickt und schmeisst es entzwei
und schmäht doch, schmied ich
Horn Call ihm nicht.

Horn Call SIEGFRIED

Hoiho! Hoiho!
Hau ein! Hau ein!
Friss ihn! Friss ihn,
den Fratzenschmied!

MIME
Fort mit dem Tier!
Was taugt mir der Bär?

SIEGFRIED
Zu zwei komm ich,
dich besser zu zwicken:
Brauner, frag nach dem Schwert!

MIME
He! Lass das Wild!
Dort liegt die Waffe:
fertig fegt ich sie heut.

SIEGFRIED
So fährst du heute noch heil!

and Alberich's ring
would then be my own.
One sword is fit for the deed,
and Nothung only will do,
when Siegfried wields it in
  war.
But I cannot forge it,
Nothung, the sword.
[he continues, unenthusiastically, to
hammer the sword]
Wearisome trouble!
Toil without end!
The finest sword
that ever I forged,
it will not serve
for the crucial deed.
I tinker and clinker away,
just to humour the boy, –
one blow, he breaks it in bits,
and scolds me, work as I will.
[he drops the hammer]

Mime (or Mimir), the old smith
and spirit of the forest, lives on
in names of some German towns,
such as Meiningen, Minden,
Münster and Memlingen.

SIEGFRIED [enters boisterously from the
forest, with a bear on a rope]
Hoiho! Hoiho!
Bear down on him!
Crunch him, munch him,
the tinker smith!
[Mime runs to hide behind the anvil]

Wagner knew how to make a bear
growl – he gives the double
basses rapid chromatic semiquavers, corkscrewing around
bottom F.

MIME
Out with the beast!
Who wants a big bear?

In his prose draft of May 1851
Wagner wrote: 'Siegfried arrives
from the forest; he has bridled
a wolf.'

SIEGFRIED
My friend joins me,
the better to plague you.
Bruin, ask for our sword!

MIME
Out with that beast!
There lies your weapon,
forged and finished for you.

SIEGFRIED
Then you are safe for today.
[he releases the bear with a stroke on the
back]

Lauf, Brauner,

Horn Call (reversed) dich brauch ich nicht *mehr*!

MIME
Wohl leid ich's gern,
erlegst du Bären:
was bringst du lebend
die Braunen heim?

SIEGFRIED
Nach bessrem Gesellen sucht ich,
als daheim mir einer sitzt;
im tiefen Walde mein Horn
liess ich hallend da ertönen:
ob sich froh mir gesellte
ein guter Freund,

Horn Call das frug ich mit dem Ge*tön*!
Aus dem Busche kam ein Bär,
der hörte mir brummend zu;
er gefiel mir besser als du,
doch bessre fänd ich wohl noch!
Mit dem zähen Baste
zäumt ich ihn da,
dich, Schelm, nach dem Schwerte

Horn Call (reversed) zu *frag*en.

MIME
Ich schuf die Waffe scharf,
ihrer Schneide wirst du dich freun.

SIEGFRIED
Horn Call Was frommt seine helle Schneide,
Siegfried ist der Stahl nicht hart und fest!
Hei! was ist das
Siegfried für müss'ger Tand!
Den schwachen Stift
Adventure nennst du ein Schwert?

Das hast du die Stücken,
schändlicher Stümper:
hätt ich am Schädel
dir sie zerschlagen!
Soll mich der Prahler
länger noch prellen?
Giants Schwatzt mir von *Rie*sen
und rüstigen Kämpfen,
von kühnen Taten
und tüchtiger Wehr;
will Waffen mir schmieden,

Run, bruin,
and thanks for your help.

MIME
Kill all the bears
you want, and welcome!
But must you bring me
the brutes alive?

SIEGFRIED
I wanted a better comrade
than the one who sits right here.
I called for him with my horn,
and the forest gave its answer.
I had hoped I should meet
with a faithful friend:
my music summoned a mate.
From the bushes broke a bear,
who growled as I blew my horn;
but I liked him better than you,
though better ones would I find.
With a rugged rope
I bridled the beast,
who'd see that the sword was
    delivered.

MIME
I made the weapon sharp,
and the steel will startle your eyes.

SIEGFRIED
What use is the steely sharpness,
if it is not tough and true?
Look, what a trashy
toy is this?
This paltry pin –
pass for a sword?
[he smashes it on the anvil]
Look, here are the pieces,
blundering bungler!
Next time your skull
shall serve for an anvil.
Must the false friend
forever deceive me?
Babbling of monsters
and marvellous battles,
of deeds of daring
and excellent arms,
of wonderful weapons

The bear exits, pursued by the
Horn Call motif in reverse.

Siegfried's indecorum is softened,
to a certain extent, by his flashes
of homespun humour.

Siegfried smashes the sword on
the anvil; by the end of the act he
will have smashed the anvil with
his sword.

(Adventure) | *(Giants)* | Schwerte schaffen;
rühmt seine Kunst,
als könnt er was Rechts:
nehm ich zur Hand nun,
was er gehämmert,
mit einem Griff
zergreif ich den Quark!
Wär mir nicht schier
zu schäbig der Wicht,
ich zerschmiedet' ihn selbst
mit seinem Geschmeid,
den alten albernen Alp!

Adventure | Des *Är*gers dann hätt ich ein End!

MIME
Nun tobst du wieder wie toll:
dein Undank, traun, ist arg!
Mach ich dem bösen Buben

Forge | nicht alles gleich zu *best*,
was ich ihm Gutes schuf,
vergisst er gar zu schnell!

Adventure | Willst du denn nie ge*den*ken,
was ich dich lehrt' vom Danke?
Dem sollst du willig gehorchen,
der je sich wohl dir erwies.

Forge | Das willst du wieder nicht *hör*en!
Doch speisen magst du wohl?
Vom Spiesse bring ich den Braten:
versuchtest du gern den Sud?

Adventure | Für dich sott ich ihn *gar*.

SIEGFRIED
Braten briet ich mir selbst:

Forge | deinen Sudel sauf all*ein*!

MIME
Das ist nun der Liebe
schlimmer Lohn!
Das der Sorgen
schmählicher Sold!

Crocodile | *Als* zullendes Kind
zog ich dich auf,
wärmte mit Kleiden
den kleinen Wurm:
Speise und Trank

he would make me,
puffed up with pride
and proud of his tricks.
But when I handle
what he has hammered,
the merest flicker
shatters the stuff.
Were not the rogue
too mean for my wrath,
I would melt him alive
along with his trash,
the doddering fool of a dwarf.
My anger then might have an end.
[flings himself down on a stone seat, while
Mime keeps out of his way]

MIME
You lost your temper again,
ungrateful boorish boy.
For this unpleasant stripling
is very hard to please.
The good things I have done,
he chooses to forget.
Why will you not remember
that children must be thankful!
Be grateful to your old guardian,
whose dearest darling you are.
You are not paying attention!
So food is what you want?
I'll fetch some flesh I have roasted;
I'll bring you a bowl of broth,
a brave succulent brew.
[Siegfried knocks the meat and bowl out of
Mime's hands]

Violas and cellos mock Mime's culinary efforts with their *col legno* accompaniment (playing the strings with the wooden part of the bow), while low clarinets trill their amused comments.

SIEGFRIED
Meat I roast for myself.
Slobber your own slops alone!

MIME
Thus a doting father
is denied!
Shameful payment
for all my pains!
Once you were my babe,
I was your nurse,
swaddled in linen
the sweet little boy,
gave you to eat,

Mime's 'sobbing' acciaccaturas (very short notes, sounded almost simultaneously with the main note) are designed to elicit Siegfried's sympathy. They only arouse his anger.

(Forge)	*(Crocodile)*	trug ich dir zu,
		hütete dich
		wie die eigne Haut.
		Und wie du erwuchsest,
		wartet ich dein;
		dein Lager schuf ich,
		dass leicht du schliefst.
		Dir schmiedet ich Tand
	Horn Call	und ein tönend *Horn*;
		dich zu erfreun,
		müht ich mich froh.
		Mit klugem Rate
		riet ich dir klug,
		mit lichtem Wissen
		lehrt ich dich Witz.
		Sitz ich daheim
		in Fleiss und Schweiss,
		nach Herzenslust
		schweifst du umher.
	Crocodile	*Für* dich nur in Plage,
		in Pein nur für dich
		verzehr ich mich alter
		armer Zwerg!
	Grief	Und aller *Last*en
	Grief	ist das nun mein *Lohn*,
		dass der hastige Knabe
		mich quält und hasst!

Adventure

SIEGFRIED
Vieles lehrtest du, Mime,
und manches lernt ich von dir;
doch was du am liebsten mich
    lehrtest,
zu lernen gelang mir nie:

Forge wie ich dich leiden könnt.
Trägst du mir Trank
und Speise herbei,
der Ekel speist mich allein;
schaffst du ein leichtes
Lager zum Schlaf,
der Schlummer wird mir da
    schwer;
willst du mich weisen,
witzig zu sein,

Adventure gern *bleib* ich taub und dumm.
Seh ich dir erst
mit den Augen zu,
zu übel erkenn ich,

Forge was alles du tust.

gave you to drink,
cherished the child
as I cherish myself.
And as you grew up,
I waited on you,
made soft your bed
for a cosy sleep.
I shaped you some toys
and a tuneful horn,
eager to please,
eager to plod.
With cunning wit
I counselled you well,
with lucid learning
I schooled your mind.
Sitting at home,
I toil and moil,
while you go
and wander at will.
I work and I worry
and put myself out,
withered and wearied:
poor old dwarf!
What do I get
for my labour of love?
An impertinent urchin's
harsh words and hate!

SIEGFRIED
Much you've lectured me, Mime,
and much have I learnt from you;
but what you would best like to
    teach me,
I never can learn from you:
how to endure your sight.
When you bring food,
and when you bring drink,
I feed off loathing alone;
when you prepare
my bed for the night,
I sleep on a bed of
    nails;
when you would school me,
sharpen my wits,
would I were deaf and dumb.
You make me sick,
when I look at you,
to see that ill-done is
whatever you do.

(Forge) Seh ich dich stehn,
gangeln und gehn,
knicken und nicken,
mit den Augen zwicken:
Adventure beim Genick möcht ich
den Nicker packen,
den Garaus geben
dem garstgen Zwicker!
So lernt ich, Mime, dich
Adventure   leiden!
Bist du nun weise,
so hilf mir wissen,
Adventure worüber umsonst ich sann:
in den Wald lauf ich,
dich zu verlassen,
wie kommt das, kehr ich zurück?
Alle Tiere sind
mir teurer als du:
Baum und Vogel,
die Fische im Bach,
lieber mag ich sie
leiden als dich:
wie kommt das nun, kehr ich
     zurück?
Longing Bist du klug, so tu mir's *kund*.

MIME
Mein Kind, das lehrt dich kennen,
wie lieb ich am Herzen dir lieg.

SIEGFRIED
Ich kann dich ja nicht leiden,
Forge vergiss das nicht so *leicht*!

MIME
Das ist deine Wildheit schuld,

Longing die du, Böser, bändgen sollst.
Jammernd verlangen Junge
nach ihrer Alten Nest;
Longing Liebe ist das Ver*lang*en:
So lechzest du auch nach mir,
so liebst du auch deinen Mime –
so musst du ihn lieben!
Was dem Vöglein ist der Vogel,

wenn er im Nest es nährt,
eh das flügge mag fliegen:
das ist dir kindschem Spross

Look at you now:
you bend and you bow,
winking and slinking,
with your eyelids blinking –
by the neck I want
to seize the goblin,
and end for ever
his loathsome twitching!
Such is the love you have taught
   me.
If you are clever,
then try and teach me
one thing I cannot make out:
in the far forest,
longing to leave you, –
what is it makes me come back?
Every beast I meet
is better than you.
Trees and birds
and the fish in the brook
mean much more to me,
Mime, than you.
What is it that makes me come
   back?
Are you wise, so tell me why!

MIME
My child, this ought to show you,
how closely I cling to your heart.

SIEGFRIED
I said, I can't abide you,
so just remember that!

MIME
That comes from your hot young
   blood.
Do control it, wayward lad!
Fledglings are always fretting
for their own parents' nest:
love is the name of this fretting;
and so do you fret for me,
and so do you love your Mime,
and must always love him!
What the mother bird is to young
   ones,
nursing them in the nest,
and before they can flutter,
such to you, dearest child,

Wagner resurrects two old German verbs: 'gangeln', to walk unsteadily, like toddlers or infirm people; and 'knicken', to hobble with bent knees.

Siegfried's oafish behaviour irritates Mime, as it irritates us. It should be remembered that he had to grow up without a father's guidance and mother's care. Wagner, too, could be intolerant and tactless. In *Mein Leben* he states that he could not remember his mother ever having cuddled him.

der kundig sorgende Mime –
das muss er dir sein!

SIEGFRIED
Ei, Mime, bist du so witzig,

Longing so lass mich eines noch *wiss*en!

Liebesnot Es *sang*en die Vöglein
so selig im Lenz,
das eine lockte das andre:
du sagtest selbst,
da ich's wissen wollt,

Longing *das* wären Männchen und
Weibchen.
Sie kosten so lieblich
und liessen sich nicht;
sie bauten ein Nest
und brüteten drin:
da flatterte junges
Geflügel auf,
und beide pflegten der Brut.

Liebesnot So *ruh*ten im Busch
auch Rehe gepaart,
selbst wilde Füchse und Wölfe:
Nahrung brachte
zum Neste das Männchen,
das Weibchen säugte die Welpen.
Da lernt ich wohl,
was Liebe sei:
der Mutter entwand ich
die Welpen nie.
Wo hast du nun, Mime,
dein minniges Weibchen,
dass ich es Mutter nenne?

MIME
Was ist dir, Tor?
Ach, bist du dumm!
Bist doch weder Vogel noch Fuchs?

SIEGFRIED

Crocodile ... *Das* zullende Kind
zogest du auf,
wärmtest mit Kleiden
den kleinen Wurm ...
Wie kam dir aber
der kindische Wurm?
Du machtest wohl gar
ohne Mutter mich?

is wise, considerate Mime,
and must always be!

SIEGFRIED
Well then, my sharp-witted Mime,
there's something else you can
    teach me:
I heard the birds singing
so sweetly in spring,
each one alluring the other;
you said yourself,
when I asked you why,
that they were wives and their
    husbands.
They chirped and they courted,
in couples they cooed;
they then built a nest
and brooded inside,
and soon tiny fledglings
would flutter about;
the parents cared for their young.
So slept in the woods
the deer side by side,
and savage wolves and foxes.
Food was found
by the young ones' father,
while mother suckled the litter.
And there I learned
what love is like;
no cub from the mother
I ever took.
Now answer me, Mime,
where is your dear consort,
that I may call her mother?

MIME
What do you mean?
Don't be a fool!
You are not a bird or a fox!

SIEGFRIED
Once I was your babe,
you were my nurse,
swaddled in linen
the little boy ...
Now tell me, how
did you get the sweet child?
Perhaps you have made me
without a wife?

Wagner found Mime's character a
source of scorn and amusement.
He wrote to Frau Ritter, his moth-
erly confidante: 'Give my best
regards to Julie and tell her that
Siegfried is progressing well. Alas,
a blot of ink has found its way on
to the beautiful portfolio. Must be
Mime's fault.'

A flute illustrates the fluttering of
the 'tiny fledglings' with its flitting
semiquavers.

The untutored youth reveals
innate wit ('Mutterwitz'). He
mocks Mime by quoting the
dwarf's own 'Crocodile' tune;
then he alludes to Mime's
fiendish aspect by insinuating that
the dwarf had fabricated a child
(Siegfried) without a mother.

MIME
Glauben sollst du,
was ich dir sage:
ich bin dir Vater
und Mutter zugleich.

SIEGFRIED

Adventure Das *lügst du*, garstiger Gauch!
Wie die Jungen den Alten
   gleichen,
das hab ich mir glücklich ersehn.
Nun kam ich zum klaren Bach:
da erspäht ich die Bäum'
und Tier' im Spiegel;
Sonn' und Wolken,
wie sie nur sind,

Siegfried im Glitzer erschienen sie gleich.
Das sah ich denn auch

Wälsungen mein eigen Bild;
ganz anders als du

Forge dünkt ich mir da:
so glich wohl der Kröte
ein glänzender Fisch;
doch kroch nie ein Fisch aus der
   Kröte!

MIME
Greulichen Unsinn

Longing⎤ kramst du da aus!

SIEGFRIED
Siehst du, nun fällt
auch selbst mir ein,
was zuvor umsonst ich besann;
wenn zum Wald ich laufe,
dich zu verlassen,
wie das kommt, kehr ich doch
   heim?
Von dir erst muss ich erfahren,
wer Vater und Mutter mir sei!

MIME
Was Vater! Was Mutter!
Müssige Frage!

SIEGFRIED

Adventure⎤ So muss ich dich *fass*en,
um was zu wissen:

MIME
You can trust me.
This is the truth, boy:
I am your father
and mother as well.

SIEGFRIED
You lie, repulsive old wretch!
All the young ones look like their
   parents,
and that I found out for myself.
One day, in the crystal brook,
I observed all the trees
and forest creatures,
clouds and sunlight,
just as they are,
all mirrored below in the brook.
And there in that brook
I saw myself,
but I did not look
like an old dwarf.
No reptile resembles
a glistening fish,
nor fish ever dropped from a
   reptile.

MIME
Horrible nonsense!
How you go on!

SIEGFRIED
Coming to think,
now I can see
what before I could not make out:
when I fly to the forest,
longing to leave you,
do you know why I come
   back?
From you I must discover
whose kindred, whose creature I
   am.

MIME
What kindred? What creature?
Meaningless question!

SIEGFRIED [seizes Mime by the throat]
Then out of your throat
the truth shall be throttled.

Siegfried's mother, Sieglinde, also
saw herself reflected in the
waters of a brook when she discovered her similarity to Siegmund (*Walküre*, Act I).

(Adventure) gutwillig
erfahr ich doch nichts!
So musst ich alles
ab dir trotzen:
kaum das Reden
hätt ich erraten,
entwand ich's mit Gewalt
nicht dem Schuft!
Heraus damit,
räudiger Kerl!
Wer ist mir Vater und Mutter?

MIME
Ans Leben gehst du mir schier!
Nun lass! Was zu wissen dich geizt,
Forge erfahr es, ganz wie ich's weiss.
O undankbares,
arges Kind!
Jetzt hör, wofür du mich hassest!

Nicht bin ich Vater
noch Vetter dir,
und dennoch verdankst du mir
dich!
Ganz fremd bist du mir,
dem einzigen Freund;
aus Erbarmen allein
barg ich dich hier:
nun hab ich lieblichen Lohn!
Was verhofft ich Tor mir auch
Wälsung Ordeal   *Sieglinde*   *Dank*?
Einst lag wimmernd ein Weib
Wälsung Ordeal da draussen im wilden Wald:

Sieglinde zur Höhle half ich ihr her,
Liebesnot am warmen Herd sie zu hüten.
Ein Kind trug sie im Schosse;
traurig gebar sie's hier;
sie wand sich hin und her,
ich half, so gut ich konnt.
Liebesnot   *Wälsung Ordeal*   *Siegfried* Gross war die *Not*! Sie starb,
doch Siegfried, der genas.

SIEGFRIED
Wälsung Ordeal So starb meine Mutter an mir?

MIME
Meinem Schutz übergab sie dich:
Wälsung Ordeal ich schenkt ihn gern dem *Kind*.

Willingly
you never will tell.
Now I shall make you
answer truly.
Even speech
I would not have learned,
if I had not wrung it out
of the rogue.
Come out with it,
slippery slob:
who are my father and mother?

MIME
You choke me almost to death!
Leave off! You are anxious to know –
alright, I'll tell you the truth.
Ungrateful child,
abusive boy,
you hate me, when you should love
   me.
I'm not your father,
not kin of yours;
your life, child, you owe to my
   love.
An alien to me,
but I am your friend;
it is pity alone
harbours you here:
and what reward do I reap?
Not gratitude, fool that I
   am.
Once a woman lay sick
out there, where the woods are
   wild.
I helped her home to this cave,
this hearth gave cover and comfort.
A babe stirred in her body;
sorrowful was the birth.
She writhed in wretched pain;
I gave what help I could.
She died,
but Siegfried, he survived.

SIEGFRIED
She died so that I might have life?

MIME
She committed you to my care;
I gladly took the child.

Even children of loving parents
often find it difficult to see what
they are supposed to be grateful
for.

Those distressing events are represented by their corresponding
motifs, Sieglinde and Wälsung
Ordeal.

Plaintive Liebesnot motifs, played
first by clarinets, then by oboe,
cor anglais and again by clarinets,
give this passage a sombre ring of
plausibility. For once, Mime is not
dissembling.

Was hat sich Mime gemüht,
was gab sich der Gute für Not!

Crocodile *Forge* *Als* zullendes *Kind*
zog ich dich auf –

SIEGFRIED

Wälsung Ordeal Mich dünkt, des ge*dach*test du
    schon!
Siegfried Jetzt *sag: w*oher heiss ich
    Siegfried?

MIME

So, hiess mich die Mutter,
möcht ich dich heiseen:
Als *Siegfried* würdest
du stark und schön.
Forge *Ich* wärmte mit Kleiden
Crocodile den kleinen Wurm –

SIEGFRIED

Wälsung Ordeal Nun *mel*de, wie hiess meine
    Mutter?

MIME

Das weiss ich wahrlich kaum!
Crocodile *Forge* *Spei*se und *Trank*
Crocodile trug ich dir zu –
Wälsung Ordeal

SIEGFRIED

Den Namen sollst du mir nennen!

MIME

Entfiel er mir wohl? Doch halt!
Sieglinde mochte sie heissen,
Forge die dich in Sorge mir *gab*.
Crocodile *Ich* hütete dich
Wälsung Ordeal wie die eigne *Haut* –

SIEGFRIED

Dann frag ich, wie hiess mein
    Vater?

MIME

Den hab ich nie gesehn.

What love was lavished on you!
How pleasantly Mime was
    plagued!
Once you were my babe,
I was your nurse –

SIEGFRIED
Again and again and again!

Now say, why am I called
    Siegfried?

MIME
Your mother's fond bidding –
so should I name you.
As Siegfried should you
grow fine and fair.
I swaddled in linen
the sweet little boy –

SIEGFRIED
And what was the name of my
    mother?

MIME
I scarcely know her name.
I gave you to eat,
gave you to drink –

SIEGFRIED
Her name! The name of my
    mother!

MIME
It slipped from my mind. But wait!
Sieglinde – possibly – surely!
She turned you over to me.
I minded the mite
as I mind myself –

SIEGFRIED
Now tell me, who was my father?

MIME
Him I have never seen.

'I shall have to see how to tell
Siegfried tomorrow morning that
his mother is dead,' Wagner wrote
in a letter in autumn 1856.

In *Das Lied vom hürnen Seyfrid*,
one of Wagner's sources, the
dwarf informs Siegfried that
both his parents were still alive.
He gives their names as King
Sieghardus and noble Adelgunde.

SIEGFRIED
Doch die Mutter nannte den
   Namen?

(Wälsung Ordeal)

MIME
Erschlagen sei er,
das sagte sie nur;
dich Vaterlosen
behahl sie mir da.
Und wie du er*wuchs*est,
wartet ich dein;
dein Lager schuf ich,
dass leicht du schliefst –

Crocodile   *Forge*

SIEGFRIED
Still mit dem alten
Staren*lied*!
Soll ich der Kunde glauben,
hast du mir nichts gelogen,
so lass mich Zeichen sehn!

Longing

MIME
Was soll dir's noch bezeugen?

SIEGFRIED
Dir glaub ich nicht mit dem Ohr,
dir glaub ich nur mit dem Aug':
welch Zeichen zeugt für dich?

Brooding   *Sword*   *Forge*

MIME

Das gab mir deine Mutter:
für Mühe, Kost und Pflege
liess sie's als schwachen Lohn.
Sieh her, ein zerbrochnes Schwert!
Dein Vater, sagte sie, führt' es,

Sword
Horn Call

als im letzten Kampf er *er*lag.

SIEGFRIED
Und diese Stücken
sollst du mir schmieden:
dann schwing ich mein rechtes
   Schwert!
Auf! Eile dich, Mime!
Mühe dich rasch;
kannst du was Rechts,
nun zeig deine Kunst!

Adventure

SIEGFRIED
But my mother spoke of my
    father?

MIME
That he was murdered,
was all that she said.
The orphan boy
she entrusted to me.
And as you grew up,
I waited on you,
made soft your bed
for a cosy sleep –

SIEGFRIED
Spare me that same old
starling song!
Shall I believe your story?
If you are not a liar,
you must produce some proof.

MIME
What proof would win you over?

SIEGFRIED
I trust you not with my ears,
I trust you but with my eyes.
What proof can you produce?

MIME [shows him two fragments of a
broken sword]
I got these from your mother.
For feeding, toil and trouble
was this the paltry pay:
look here at this splintered sword!
She said the sword was your
    father's,
when that fatal fight was his last.

SIEGFRIED
And you shall forge
these fragments together,
and mine be my father's
    sword!
So to your work, Mime,
waste no more time!
Now you can show
your cunning craft.

The unknown father plays an
important part in Wagner's works.
Siegmund, Sieglinde, Tristan, Parsifal – all are fatherless. As for
Wagner himself, he was never
quite certain who his father was,
police official Carl Friedrich Wil-
helm Wagner, or Ludwig Geyer,
the actor and poet whom his
mother had married after her husband's death.

The motifs of Brooding, Sword
and Forge reveal Mime's preoccu-
pation with his dilemma – who is
to forge those unforgeable fragments?

Siegfried feels that this will be his
rightful weapon. The Sword motif
shifts into his Horn Call.

(Adventure) Sword

Täusche mich nicht
mit schlechtem Tand:
den Trümmern allein
trau ich was zu!
Find ich dich faul,
fügst du dich schlecht,
flickst du mit Flausen
den festen Stahl,
dir Feigem fahr ich zu Leib,
das Fegen lernst du von mir!
Denn heute noch, schwör ich,
Sword
will ich das Schwert;
die Waffe gewinn ich noch heut!

MIME
Was willst du noch heut mit dem
Schwert?

SIEGFRIED
Freedom
Aus dem Wald fort
in die Welt ziehn:
nimmer kehr ich zurück!
Wie ich froh bin,
dass ich frei ward,
nichts mich bindet und zwingt!
Adventure
Mein *Vater* bist du nicht;
in der Ferne bin ich heim;
dein Herd ist nicht mein Haus,
meine Decke nicht dein Dach.
Freedom
Wie der Fisch froh
in der Flut schwimmt,
wie der Fink frei
sich davonschwingt:
flieg ich von hier,
flute davon,
wie der Wind übern Wald
weh ich dahin,
dich, Mime, nie wieder zu sehn!

MIME
Halte! Halte!
Halte! Wohin?
He! Siegfried!
Freedom
Siegfried! He!

Da stürmt er hin!
Ring
Nun sitz ich da:

Trick me no more
with worthless trash.
These splinters alone
serve for my sword.
If you are slack,
if you are slow,
or if you damage
the stalwart steel,
then, coward, look to your skin:
I'll burnish it brighter than steel!
I swear that today
I shall have my sword.
I'll win me that weapon today!

MIME
But why must you have it today?

SIEGFRIED
From the forest
to the wide world,
never more to return.
Full of joy now,
fancy-free now,
nothing fetters me here.
My father you are not,
and my home is far away;
your hearth is not my house,
and your roof not my repose.
As the fish flits
in the river,
as the finch flies
over hilltops,
so shall I fly
far, far away,
with the wind through the woods
wending my way:
then, Mime, see, I shall be free!
[he rushes out into the forest]

MIME
Stop, boy! Stop, boy!
Come back to me!
Hey, Siegfried!
Siegfried, hey! [he looks puzzled, as
Siegfried storms away, then he seats himself
behind the anvil]
Away he storms,
and I sit here.

The *Thidrek Saga* told Wagner
that the young Sigurd (Siegfried),
as an apprentice smith, was given
to victorious fisticuffs with his fellow apprentices. *Das Lied vom
hürnen Seyfrid* goes further:
there, Seyfrid 'takes his master by
the scruff of his neck and throws
him on the ground.'

The *Volsunga Saga* shows a more
considerate youngster. He tells
the smith, 'Much hast thou lost,
and exceeding evil have thy kinsmen been. But now make a
sword as that none can be made
like unto it; so that I may do great
deeds therewith.'

A mini-aria, to be treasured for its
charm and its rarity.

Schopenhauer pencilled 'Empö-
render Undank' ('scandalous
ingratitude') in the margin of his
copy.

(Ring) zur alten Not
hab ich die neue;
Forge *Brooding* vernagelt bin ich nun *ganz*!
Wie helf ich mir jetzt?
Dragon Wie halt ich ihn *fest*?
Wie führ ich den Huien
Grief zu Fafners *Nest*?
Wie füg ich die Stücken
des tückischen Stahls?
Keines Ofens Glut
glüht mir die echten:
keines Zwergen Hammer
zwingt mir die harten.
Liebe-Tragik Des *Nib*lungen Neid,
Not und Schweiss
Wanderer nietet mir Nothung *nicht*,
schweisst das Schwert nicht zu
ganz!

To crown my cares
comes added trouble.
I'm snared, enmeshed in my trap.
What help for me now?
How hold the boy here?
How lead the wild truant
to Fafner's lair?
How fragile those fragments,
how stubborn the steel!
Not the fiercest heat
helps me to fuse them,
nor can this my hammer
humble their hardness.
Nor Nibelung hate,
sweat nor toil
ever make Nothung new,
ever forge me this sword!
[he crouches in despair behind the anvil]

In Wagner's draft of 1853 Mime
succeeds in calling Siegfried back.
He pretends that Sieglinde had
charged him not to send her son
out into the world before he has
learned the meaning of fear.
Siegfried, however, decides that
the world outside, not Mime,
shall teach him, and storms away.

i. Akt: 2. Szene

WANDERER

Wanderer

Heil dir, weiser Schmied!
Dem wegmüden Gast
gönne hold
Treasure des Hauses *Herd*!

MIME

Wer ist's, der im wilden
Walde mich sucht?
Wer verfolgt mich im öden Forst?

WANDERER

Wanderer
*Wand*rer heisst mich die Welt;
weit wandert' ich schon:
auf der Erde Rücken
rührt' ich mich viel.

MIME

Forge So rühre dich fort
und raste nicht hier,
nennt dich Wandrer die Welt!

WANDERER

Gastlich ruht' ich bei Guten,
Wanderer Gaben gönnten viele *mir*:
denn Unheil fürchtet,
wer unhold ist.

MIME

Unheil wohnte
immer bei mir:
willst du dem Armen es mehren?

WANDERER

Viel erforscht' ich,

Act I: Scene 2

[The Wanderer (Wotan) enters Mime's cave
from the forest. He wears a dark blue cloak
and he uses his spear as a staff. His large,
broad-brimmed hat covers his missing eye.]

WANDERER
Greetings, worthy smith!
A way-weary guest
seeks to rest,
so grant him repose.

Four trombones, trumpet and bass
trumpet endow the Wanderer
motif with sombre authority.

MIME
Who is it that tracks me
in my retreat?
Who discovered my forest lair?

Immediately after the 'Wanderer'
chords we hear the Treasure
motif, which hints at Mime's pre-
occupation. He really is not at
leisure, just now, to entertain
strangers.

WANDERER
Wanderer, that is my name.
Far, far have I fared;
on the earth's vast surface
much have I moved.

Wotan has wandered a long way
since those heady days of *Rheingold* (Scene 4), when he took
possession of Walhall. Now he
seeks temporary shelter in Mime's
cave.

MIME
Then move from this place
and wander away –
wandering is your delight.

In the early prose draft of May
1851, Mime threatens 'to chastise
the impudent guest'.

WANDERER
Good folk grant me their shelter,
many offer gifts to me.
Bad luck will follow,
where men are false.

MIME
Bad luck always
lives in this place.
Must you augment my misfortune?

WANDERER
Much I studied

erkannte viel:
wichtges konnt' ich
manchem künden,
manchem wehren,
was ihn mühte,
Treasure   nagende Herzens*not.*

MIME
Spürtest du klug
und erspähtest du viel,
hier brauch ich nicht Spürer noch
   Späher.
Einsam will ich
und einzeln sein,
Lungerern lass ich den Lauf.

WANDERER
Mancher wähnte,
weise zu sein,
nur was ihm not tat,
wusste er nicht;
was ihm frommte,
liess ich erfragen:
lohnend lehrt' ihn mein Wort.

MIME
Grief   *Müss*ges Wissen
wahren manche:
Forge   ich weiss mir grade ge*nug.*
Mir genügt mein Witz,
ich will nicht mehr:
Treaty   dir Weisem weis ich den *Weg*!

WANDERER
Wanderer   Hier sitz ich am *Herd*
und setze mein Haupt
Treaty   der Wissenswette zum *Pfand.*
mein Kopf ist dein,
du hast ihn erkiest,
entfrägst du mir nicht,
was dir frommt,
Forge   lös ich's mit Lehren nicht ein.

MIME

Brooding   Wie werd ich den Lauernden los?
Treaty   Verfänglich muss ich ihn fragen.
Dein Haupt pfänd ich
für den Herd:

and much I saw.
Words of wisdom
can I render.
I can save men
from their sorrows,
healing their harassed hearts.

MIME
Prowl where you will,
and prophesy too,
I need neither prophets nor
   prowlers.
Lonely am I,
so let me be.
Wanderer, be on your way!

WANDERER
Some there are
who think they are wise,
but what they need
they often neglect.
Apt advice
is theirs for the asking,
wisdom is their reward.

Wagner's original plan was for the
Wanderer to ask Mime to enchant
him with his wisdom, while Mime
wishes the intruder speedily
away. Siegfried might be back at
any moment, and it would not do
for the lad to glean information
which Mime wants to withhold
from him.

MIME
Needless wisdom,
wasted knowledge,
for I know all that I need.
I have wit to spare,
I want no more,
so, wise man, there lies your way!

WANDERER
I sit by your hearth
and stake my own head,
as pledge in a wager of wits.
My head is yours,
to have and to hold,
unless I can render
apt advice,
rightly redeeming the pledge.

The present Wotan is less self-
centred than the god in *Rheingold*. There he wagered Freia for
Walhall. Here he stakes his own
head.

MIME [open-mouthed, timorous,
shrinking back]
How can I get rid of the rogue?
With art and guile must I ask him.
You staked your head
for my hearth.

nun sorg, es sinnig zu lösen!
Drei der Fragen
stell ich mir frei.

WANDERER
Forge + Treaty Dreimal muss ich's treffen.
Brooding

MIME
Du rührtest dich viel
auf der Erde Rücken,
Forge *Brooding* die Welt durchwandertst du weit:

nun sage mir schlau,
welches Geschlecht
tagt in der Erde Tiefe?

WANDERER
In der Erde Tiefe
Forge tagen die *Nib*elungen:
Nibelheim ist ihr Land.
Schwarzalben sind sie;
Schwarz-Alberich
Ring hütet' als Herrscher sie einst!
Eines Zauberringes
zwingende Kraft
Treasure zähmt' ihm das fleissige *Volk*.
Reicher Schätze
schimmernden Hort
Arrogance häuften sie *ihm*:
Treaty der sollte die Welt ihm gewinnen.

Forge *Brooding* Zum zweiten was frägst du, Zwerg?

MIME
Viel, Wanderer,
weisst du mir
Forge *Brooding* aus der Erde Nabelnest:
Nun sage mir schlicht,
welches Geschlecht
ruht auf der Erde Rücken?

WANDERER
Auf der Erde Rücken
Giants *Giants* wuchtet der *Rie*sen Geschlecht.
Riesenheim ist ihr Land.
Fasolt und Fafner,
der Rauhen Fürsten,
neideten Nibelungs Macht;

Perhaps your prowess will prosper.
Three are the problems
that I shall pose.

WANDERER
Three times must I hit it.

MIME
You've journeyed far
on the earth's vast surface,
you've wandered much in the
    world.
Now show what you know:
which is the race
dwells in the earth's deep caverns?

WANDERER
In the earth's deep caverns
dwell the dark Nibelungen.
Nibelheim is their land.
Schwarzalben are they.
Schwarz-Alberich
once was their guardian and guide.
By his magic ring's
omnipotent spell
he now controls all his tribe.
Precious riches,
rarest of hoards
he had piled up,
to conquer the world for his
    kingdom.
Now ask your next question, dwarf!

MIME
Yes, Wanderer,
much you know
of the earth's deep navel-nest.
Now answer me straight:
which is the race
dwells on its spacious surface?

WANDERER
On its spacious surface
clodhopping giants are found.
Riesenheim is their land.
Fasolt and Fafner
who rule the ruffians,
envied the Nibelung's might.

In the *Thidrek Saga* Wagner had
read of Welent, the master smith.
When challenged by his rival to a
sword-forging contest, Welent
staked his head, since he had no
gold to wager.

'Schwarzalben' are 'dark spirits'.

'Riesenheim' is 'giants' home'.

(Giants)
den gewaltigen Hort
gewannen sie sich,
Ring
errangen mit ihm den Ring.
Um den entbrannte
den Brüdern Streit;
Dragon
der Fasolt *fäll*te,
Treaty
als wilder Wurm
hütet nun Fafner den Hort.
Forge   *Brooding*
Die dritte Frage nun droht.

MIME
Viel, Wanderer,
weisst du mir
Forge   *Brooding*
von der Erde rauhem Rücken.
Nun sage mir wahr,
welches Geschlecht
wohnt auf wolkigen Höhn?

WANDERER
Auf wolkigen Höhn
Walhall
wohnen die *Götter*:
Walhall heisst ihr Saal.
Lichtalben sind sie;
Licht-Alberich
Wotan, waltet der Schar.
Genesis
Aus der *Welt*-Esche
weihlichstem Aste
Treaty
schuf er sich einen *Schaft*:
dorrt der Stamm,
Treaty
nie verdirbt doch der *Speer*;
Authority
mit seiner *Spitz*e
Treaty
sperrt Wotan die *Welt*.
Heilger Verträge
Treuerunen
Authority
schnitt in den Schaft er ein.
Den Haft der Welt
Treaty
hält in der *Hand*,
wer den Speer führt,
Grief
den Wotans Faust um*spann*t.
Ihm neigte sich
Ring
der *Nib*lungen Heer;
der Riesen Ge*züch*t
Authority
zähmte sein *Rat*:
Wanderer
ewig gehorchen sie alle
Treaty
des Speeres starkem *Herrn*.

The prodigious hoard
they won for themselves,
and with it also the ring,
which caused grim warfare
between the two.
Fafner slew Fasolt.
In dragon shape
Fafner now guards all that gold.
One quick-witted question
  remains.

MIME
Much, Wanderer,
much you know
of the rude earth's rugged surface.
Now answer me true:
which is the race
dwells on cloud-covered heights?

WANDERER
On cloud-covered heights
dwell the eternals.
Walhall is their home.
Lichtalben are they.
Licht-Alberich,
Wotan, rules as their lord.
From the World Ash Tree's
holiest bough
he shaped himself a shaft.
Trunks may rot,
but the spear remains true,
and with that weapon
he governs the world.
Sacrosanct runes
of trusted treaties
deep in the shaft he shaped.
The world is ruled
only by him
who commands it,
and Wotan is its lord.
Before him bows
the Nibelung host.
The giants themselves
have come to heel.
All must obey as their master
the mighty lord of the spear.
[as he strikes the ground with his spear, a
far-off thunder is heard which terrifies
Mime]

In his earlier draft Wagner provided detailed giant-lore, as fur-
nished for him in the Edda: the
race of giants, Wotan related, was
generated by frost and brought
forth by heat; he added that lately
almost 'the whole race had per-
ished at each other's hands', and
that Fafner was the sole survivor.

'Lichtalben' are 'spirits of light'.
'Licht-Alberich' is the male spirit
of light, i.e. Wotan.

In Wagner's draft Wotan explained
that one of his eyes shines as a
star in the firmament. We recall
that in *Rheingold* Wotan gave a
different reason for the loss of
one eye: he surrendered it to win
Freia for wife. In *Götterdämmerung* we shall hear yet another
version: he gave one eye to drink
from the Well of Wisdom. The
three accounts may seem contra-
dictory, but are not necessarily so.

Nun rede, weiser Zwerg:
wusst ich der Fragen Rat?

Forge   Behalte mein Haupt ich frei?

MIME
Fragen und Haupt
hast du gelöst:
nun, Wandrer, geh deines Wegs!

WANDERER
Was zu wissen dir frommt,
solltest du fragen:

Wanderer   *Treaty*   *Kun*de verbürgte mein *Kopf.*
Dass du nun nicht weisst,
was dir frommt,

Treaty   des fass ich jetzt deines als *Pfand.*

Gastlich nicht
galt mir dein Gruss,
mein Haupt gab ich
in deine Hand,
um mich des Herdes zu freun.
Nach Wettens Pflicht
pfänd ich nun dich,
lösest du drei

Treaty   der Fragen nicht leicht.

Forge   **Shuffle**   Drum frische dir, Mime, den Mut!

MIME

Forge   *Shuffle*   Lang schon *mied* ich
mein Heimatland,
lang schon schied ich

Walhall   aus der Mutter *Schoss*;
mir leuchtete Wotans Auge,

zur Höhle lugt' er herein:
vor ihm magert

Forge   mein Mutterwitz.

Shuffle   Doch *frommt* mir's nun, weise zu
sein,

Forge   Wandrer, frage denn zu!
Vielleicht glückt mir's, gezwungen
zu lösen des Zwergen Haupt.

WANDERER
Nun, ehrlicher Zwerg,

Wälsungen   sag mir zum *ersten*:

Now tell me, learned troll,
were all my answers true?
My head, is it mine to hold?

MIME
Wager and head,
both you have won.
Now, wanderer, wander away!

WANDERER
What you needed to know,
you should have asked me,
while you had hold of my head.
But you do not know
what you need,
so now I claim your head as
    pledge.
Grudgingly
you greeted me.
My head I gave
into your hand,
to rest awhile at your hearth.
By hazard's law,
now stake your life!
Answer me quick:
three questions I ask.
Show wisdom, Mime, and wit.

MIME
Long it is,
since I left my home;
very long it is,
since I was born.
But now Wotan's eye quite blinds
    me,
my cave is exposed to its blaze.
His glance withers
my mother-wit.
Yet now it were wise to be
    wise.
Wanderer, ask what you will.
Perhaps fortune will help me
to cling to my clever head.

WANDERER
Now, trustworthy dwarf,
first let me ask you:

(Wälsungen)

Wotan's Farewell   welches ist das Geschlecht,
dem Wotan schlimm sich zeigte,
und das doch das liebste ihm

Forge   *Shuffle*   lebt?

MIME
Wenig hört ich

Forge   von Helden*sip*pen;

Shuffle   der *Fra*ge doch mach ich mich frei.

Wälsungen   Die *Wäl*sungen sind
das Wunschgeschlecht,
das Wotan zeugte
und zärtlich liebte,
zeigt' er auch Ungunst ihm.
Siegmund und Sieglind
stammten von Wälse,
ein wild-verzweifeltes

Siegfried   Zwil*ling*spaar:
Siegfried zeugten sie selbst,

Forge   *Shuffle*   den stärksten Wälsungenspross.
Behalt ich, Wandrer,

Forge   zum ersten mein Haupt?

WANDERER

Forge   Wie doch genau
das Geschlecht du mir nennst:
schlau eracht ich dich Argen!
Der ersten Frage
wardst du frei.

Forge   *Brooding*   Zum zweiten nun sag mir, *Zwerg*:
ein weiser Niblung
wahret Siegfried;

Dragon   *Faf*nern soll er ihm fällen,
dass den Ring er erränge,
des Hortes Herrscher zu sein.

Welches Schwert
muss Siegfried nun schwingen,

Forge   taug es zu Fafners Tod?

MIME

Shuffle   *Noth*ung heisst

Sword   ein neidliches *Schwert*;
in einer Esche Stamm
stiess es Wotan;
dem sollt es geziemen,

Forge   der aus dem Stamm es zög.

name the name of the race
that Wotan has forsaken,
though he loves it more than his
   life.

MIME
Little I know
of heroes' kinship,
but here is my ready reply.
The Wälsungen are
that chosen race,
that Wotan fathered
and fondly cherished –
but he has cast them off.
Siegmund and Sieglind,
children of Wälse,
that love-tormented
twin-born pair.
Siegfried sprang from their love,
the lustiest Wälsung is he.
I ask you, Wanderer,
my head is still mine?

'Wälse' is Wotan.

The doom-laden Wälsungen motif
sounds positively sprightly and
innocuous when Mime sings
'Siegmund und Sieglind', just as
some 'modern' producers would
have us believe that the whole
Ring is healthy fun, sprightly and
innocuous.

WANDERER
O, you are right,
you have heard of that race.
Crafty are you and cunning.
This question you have
quickly solved.
Now try the next challenge, troll!
A subtle Niblung
shelters Siegfried,
hoping he should kill Fafner;
then the ring could be ravished
which makes him lord of the
   hoard.
Name the sword
that Siegfried must brandish,
so that Fafner will fall.

'Crafty are you and cunning,' says
Wotan, ironically. The music tells
us that he is aware of Mime's
duplicity. Wagner had used this
phrase in *Rheingold* when Fafner
informed his brother of Wotan's
duplicity: 'My trustful brother,
fool, to fall for his tricks!'

MIME [much encouraged, he rubs
his hands]
Nothung is
that nonpareil sword.
Once in an ash tree's trunk
Wotan struck it.
One man should possess it:
he who could pluck it out.

'Not' is 'need', therefore 'Nothung'
is the 'sword won in the hour of
need'.

Shuffle	Der *stärk*sten Helden
	keiner bestand's:
Sword	Siegmund, der *Kühn*e,
	konnt's allein:
	fechtend führt' er's im Streit,
Forge	bis an Wotans Speer es zer*sprang*.
	Nun verwahrt die Stücken
	ein weiser Schmied;
	denn er weiss, dass allein
	mit dem Wotansschwert
Siegfried + Shuffle	ein *kühn*es, dummes Kind,
Sword　　*Shuffle*	*Sieg*fried,den Wurm ver*sehrt*.
	Behalt ich Zwerg
	auch zweitens mein Haupt?

WANDERER

Shuffle	Der *witz*igste bist du
	unter den Weisen:
	wer käm dir an Klugheit gleich?
	Doch bist du so klug,
	den kindischen Helden
Forge	für *Zwerg*enzwecke zu nutzen,
	mit der dritten Frage
	droh ich nun!
	Sag mir, du weiser
	Waffenschmied:
Siegfried	wer wird aus den starken Stücken
	Nothung, das Schwert, wohl
Adventure	*schwei*ssen?

MIME

Adventure	Die Stücken! Das Schwert!
	O weh! Mir schwindelt!
	Was fang ich an?
	Verfluchter Stahl,
	dass ich dich gestohlen!
	Er hat mich vernagelt
Grief	in Pein und *Not*!
	Mir bleibt er hart,
	ich kann ihn nicht hämmern;
	Niet' und Löte
	lässt mich im Stich!
	Der weiseste Schmied
	weiss sich nicht Rat!
Liebe-Tragik	*Wer* schweisst nun das Schwert,
	schaff ich es nicht?
Wanderer	Das Wunder, wie soll ich's *wiss*en?

The strongest heroes
struggled in vain.
Siegmund the valiant
did the deed.
Thus he gained his own sword,
but on Wotan's spear was it split.
Its remains are kept
by a cunning smith,
for he knows that only
with Wotan's sword,
a brave and artless boy,
Siegfried, may slay the beast.
May a poor old dwarf
hang on to his head?

WANDERER [laughing]
The deepest are you
of all the deep ones!
Who could be as subtle as you?
Since you are so wise,
to use the young hero
as agent of your ambition,
let my final question
find you out.
Tell me, my artful
armourer:
you only possess the fragments –
Nothung, the sword, who shall
   forge it?

MIME
The fragments! The sword!
I'm caught, I'm crippled!
What shall I do?
Accursed steel,
that I ever stole it!
I am quite nailed down
in my hour of need.
Hard is that steel,
too hard for my hammer.
Rivet, solder,
bootless are both.
The cleverest smith
comes to his end.
Who forges a sword
I cannot forge?
Who answers what cannot be
   answered?

While Mime and the Wanderer
listen, in turn, to each other's
answers, we listeners refresh our
memories of the events under
discussion.

If Mime had listened attentively
he might have noticed the Adventure motif on the Wanderer's last
words. This would have provided
the vital clue: Siegfried is to forge
the sword.

Mime blurts out that he stole the
splinters. Yet he told Siegfried
that Sieglinde had given them to
him. Ernest Newman maintains
that Wagner's memory played him
false. In fact, Mime's two state-
ments are compatible: he lied to
Siegfried, but in his present frenzy
reveals the truth.

WANDERER

Wanderer Dreimal solltest du fragen,

dreimal stand ich dir frei:
nach eitlen Fernen
forschtest du;
Liebe-Tragik doch was zu*nächst* dir sich fand,
was dir nützt, fiel dir nicht ein.
Sword Nun ich's *er*rate,
Treaty + Forge wirst du ver*rückt*:
gewonnen hab ich
das witzige Haupt!
Jetzt, Fafners kühner Bezwinger,
Dragon hör, verfallner *Zwerg*:
Nur wer das Fürchten
Sword nie *erfuhr*,
Loge schmiedet Nothung *neu*.
Dein weises Haupt
Crisis wahre von heut:
Siegfried *ver*fallen lass ich es dem,
Loge der das Fürchten nicht ge*lernt*!

WANDERER

Thrice you asked your own
   questions,
thrice I was in your hand.
You searched for futile,
far off things;
but what concerns you alone,
what you need, that you ignored.
What I must tell you,
will drive you mad.
As prize I call for
your precious head.
So, Fafner's daring destroyer,
listen and learn your doom.
He who has never
harboured fear,
he shall forge the sword.
Your cunning head,
guard it with care!
I leave it forfeit to him
who has never harboured fear.
[He turns away, smiling, and disappears into
the forest. Mime sinks down behind the
anvil.]

Once again, the 'Fear' phrase
sounds in the cellos and double
basses.

In the draft of May 1851, Wotan
was more than fair to Mime:
'Siegfried alone shall forge his
sword. You can keep your wise
head; it is no use to me. But
guard it well from now on.
Beware lest your tongue gives
you away. Do not indulge in silly
chatter.'

Eduard Hanslick, Wagner's cen-
sorious Viennese critic, was the
model for Beckmesser, the
pedantic town clerk in Wagner's
Meistersinger. Hanslick justified
his prestige when he declared:
'What can one say of Wotan's long
scene with the dwarf? Each gives
the other three questions, and
each answers with the detailed
precision of a well-tutored can-
didate at a school examination.
The whole scene, utterly superflu-
ous from the dramatic point of
view, is an oppressive bore.'

Wotan seems to be unable or
unwilling to fulfil contractual
obligations. He withholds Freia
from the giants, the ring from the
Rhinemaidens, the power of the
sword from Siegmund, and
Mime's head from himself. Irres-
olution or prudence?

Wotan's first question concerned
the past, his second the present,
his third the future. Mime may be
expected to show his grasp of
past and present events; but the
future? Is Wotan quite fair? I think
he is: Wotan is not interested in
the answer, but shows Mime that
a mere mortal should not waste
an opportunity to obtain divine
guidance.

I. Akt: 3. Szene

Dragon *Magic Fire* MIME
Verfluchtes Licht!
Was flammt dort die Luft?
Was flackert und lackert,
was flimmert und schwirrt,
was schwebt dort und webt
und wabert umher?
Dort glimmert's und glitzt's
in der Sonne Glut!
Was säuselt und summt
und saust nun gar?
Es brummt und braust
und prasselt hieher!
Dort bricht's durch den Wald,
will auf mich zu!
Ein grässlicher Rachen
reisst sich mir auf:
der Wurm will mich fangen!
Fafner! Fafner!

Sword

Freedom SIEGFRIED

Heda, du Fauler!
Bist du nun fertig?
Schnell, wie steht's mit dem
Adventure   *Schwert*?
Wo steckt der Schmied?
Stahl er sich fort?
Hehe, Mime, du Memme!
Dragon Wo bist du? Wo birgst du *dich*?

MIME
Bist du es, Kind?
Kommst du allein?

SIEGFRIED
Adventure Hinter dem *Am*boss?
Sag, was schufest du dort?
Dragon Schärftest du mir das *Schwert*?

Act I: Scene 3

MIME [staring into the forest, trembling]
Accursed light!
The air is on fire!
What quivers and shivers,
what flashes and flares?
What flits and what floats
and flickers around?
It glistens and gleams
in the sunlight's glow!
What hisses and hums
and howls all around?
It rolls and roars
and rumbles this way!
It breaks through the trees,
rushing at me!
The maw of a monster
opens up wide:
the dragon will grab me!
Fafner! Fafner!
[he collapses behind the anvil]

SIEGFRIED [bursts through the thicket,
still off-stage]
Ho there! You dawdler!
Is the work done yet? [enters the cave]
Here, I've come for my sword.

But where's the smith?
Has he made off?
Hey, hey! Mime, you mousekin!
Where are you? Come out, I say!

MIME [from behind the anvil]
O lad, it's you!
Are you alone?

SIEGFRIED
Under the anvil?
What are you doing there?
Are you sharpening my sword?

Magic Fire and Dragon motifs
underline Mime's predicament.
Wagner the psychologist reveals
the chaos in Mime's mind.

The tam-tam (gong) reinforces
Mime's horror.

In the 1851 draft Siegfried 'enters
with the bear'. Wagner later decided to let the beast make a
more impressive entrance at the
beginning of the act.

(Dragon)		**MIME**
		Das Schwert? Das Schwert?
		Wie möcht ich's schweissen?
		Nur wer das Fürchten
Sword		nie er*fuhr*,
Loge		schmiedet Nothung *neu*.
		Zu weise ward ich
Adventure		für solches *Werk*!

SIEGFRIED
Adventure⌉ Wirst du mir reden?
Soll ich dir raten?

Loge⌉ **MIME**
Wanderer⌉ Wo nähm ich redlichen *Rat*?
Mein weises Haupt
Siegfried hab ich verwettet:
verfallen, verlor ich's an den,
Adventure der das Fürchten nicht ge*lern*t.

SIEGFRIED
Adventure⌉ Sind mir das Flausen?
Willst du mir fliehn?

MIME
Adventure⌉ Wohl flöh ich dem,
der's *Fürchten* kennt!
Forge⌉ Doch das liess ich dem Kinde zu
lehren!
Ich Dummer vergass,
was einzig gut:
Liebe zu mir
sollt' er lernen;
Loge⌉ das gelang nun leider *faul*!
Wie bring ich das Fürchten ihm
bei?

SIEGFRIED
Adventure *He!* Muss ich helfen?
Was fegtest du heut?

MIME
Um dich nur besorgt,
versank ich in Sinnen,
wie ich dich Wichtiges wiese.

SIEGFRIED
Bis unter den Sitz
warst du versunken:
was Wichtiges fandest du da?

MIME
The sword? The sword?
How could I forge it? [half to himself]
... He who has never
harboured fear,
he shall forge the sword ...
I have more sense
than to risk my neck!

Once again, the coiling 'Fear'
phrase denotes Mime's shivering
perplexity.

SIEGFRIED
Will you speak plainly?
Shall I assist you?

MIME
Where can I turn in my need?
My wise old head
here have I wagered,
and lost it as forfeit to him
who has never learnt to fear.

'Haven't I told you about the lad
who sets out to learn how to
fear? Imagine my shock when I
suddenly realized that this lad is
none other than – young
Siegfried, who wins the hoard
and wakes Brünnhilde!' (Wagner
to Uhlig, 10 May 1851)

SIEGFRIED
I know your tricks.
Don't try them on me!

MIME
Him would I fly
who harbours fear,
and that lesson you have not yet
    learned, lad.
But, fool, I forgot
the crucial thing!
Loving the dwarf
is your duty,
but alas, it all went wrong.
Now how can I make him feel
    fear?

SIEGFRIED
Answer me, Mime,
what work have you done?

MIME
On your dear behalf
I fell into musing,
how I could teach you what matters.

SIEGFRIED
You mean that you fell
under the anvil.
What matters did Mime find there?

MIME
Das Fürchten lernt ich für dich,
dass ich dich's Dummen lehre.

SIEGFRIED
Was ist's mit dem Fürchten?

MIME
Erfuhrst du's noch nie
und willst aus dem Wald
Sword + Adventure doch fort in die Welt?
Was frommte das festeste
   Schwert,
Forge blieb dir das Fürchten *fern*?

SIEGFRIED
Faulen Rat
Wälsung Ordeal erfindest du *wohl*?

MIME
Wälsung Ordeal⌉ Deiner Mutter Rat
redet aus mir;
was ich gelobte,
muss ich nun lösen:
in die listige Welt
dich nicht zu entlassen,
Loge eh du nicht das Fürchten ge*lernt*.

SIEGFRIED
Adventure⌉ *Ist's* eine Kunst,
was kenn ich sie nicht?
Heraus! Was ist's mit dem
Loge Fürch*ten*?

MIME
Loge⌉ Fühltest du nie
im finstren Wald,
bei Dämmerschein
am dunklen Ort,
wenn fern es säuselt,
summst und saust,
wildes Brummen
näher braust,
wirres Flackern
um dich flimmert,
schwellend Schwirren
zu Leib dir schwebt:
fühltest du dann nicht grieselnd
Sanctuary⌉ Grausen die Glieder dir fahen?

MIME
I found a thing they call Fear:
that is what really matters.

SIEGFRIED
Then tell me about it.

MIME
You do not know Fear,
and yet you would leave
these woods for the world?
What use is the sturdiest
    steel,
if you are free from Fear?

SIEGFRIED
Trivial trash
I'm likely to hear.

MIME
It's your mother's words,
speaking through me!
She made me promise
I should instruct you;
to a world full of wiles
I should not dispatch you,
without the experience of fear.

SIEGFRIED
Is it a skill,
why am I unskilled?
Come on and teach me what fear
    is!

MIME
Have you not felt,
in gloomy woods,
when darkness falls
in dusky glades,
a far off murmur
in your ear,
savage growling
growing near;
dazzling flashes
dart and flicker;
horror hovers
above your head:
then have you felt that gruesome
grip on your battered body,

(Loge) | *(Sanctuary)* | Glühender Schauer
schüttelt die Glieder,
in der Brust bebend und bang
berstet hämmernd das Herz?
Fühltest du das noch nicht,
das Fürchten blieb dir noch fremd.

SIEGFRIED

Sanctuary Sonderlich *selt*sam
muss das sein!
Siegfried Hart *und* fest,
Magic Fire fühl ich, steht mir das *Herz*.
Das Grieseln und Grausen,
das Glühen und Schauern,
Hitzen und Schwindeln,
Hämmern und Beben:
gern begehr ich das Bangen,
Sanctuary *sehn*end verlangt mich's der Lust!
Doch wie bringst du,
Mime, mir's bei?
Dragon Wie wärst du, Memme, mir *Meist*er?

MIME

Dragon Folge mir nur,
ich führe dich wohl:
sinnend fand ich es aus.
Ich weiss einen schlimmen Wurm,
der würgt' und schlang schon viel:
Fafner lehrt dich das Fürchten,
Sanctuary folgst du mir zu seinem *Nest.*

SIEGFRIED

Sanctuary Wo liegt er im Nest?

MIME

Sanctuary Neidhöhle
wird es genannt:
im Ost, am Ende des Walds.

SIEGFRIED

Sanctuary Dann wär's nicht weit von der Welt?

MIME

Bei Neidhöhle liegt sie ganz nah.

SIEGFRIED

Dahin denn sollst du mich
    führen:
lernt ich das Fürchten,
dann fort in die Welt!

shivers and shudders
throbbing right through you?
In your breast, bursting with dread,
wildly hammers your heart.
Till you have felt such things,
you'll be a stranger to fear.

SIEGFRIED [thoughtfully]
How very curious
that must be.
Steadfast, strong
beats my heart, just the same.
Such shivers and shudders,
such troublesome trembling,
beating and burning,
quivering and quaking, –
how I long for this terror,
could I but taste such joy!
But how will you
teach me these things?
Can such a mousekin be master?

MIME
Follow me, boy!
I find you the way;
I have worked it all out.
A deadly dragon I know,
has massacred many a man.
Fafner shows you what fear is.
I shall lead you to his lair.

SIEGFRIED
And where is this lair?

MIME
Neidhöhle,
that is its name:
due east, at the edge of the woods.

SIEGFRIED
It lies not far from the world?

MIME
Near Neidhöhle lies the big world!

SIEGFRIED
Then that is where you must take
  me.
Fear be my fellow,
then into the world!

The Sanctuary motif anticipates the moment in Act III when Siegfried will learn fear – at the sight of the slumbering Brünnhilde.

Wagner directs Mime to sing 'with quavering voice', 'quivering' and 'trembling'. He has hypnotized himself into a state of hysterical terror.

With the Sanctuary motif (oboe, cor anglais, horn) and Dragon motif (cello), Wagner gives notice of the psychological thunderbolt in Act III when Siegfried will break into Brünnhilde's sanctuary, to be greeted by her to the Dragon motif! Wagner anticipates Freud by alluding to the loving woman's devouring instinct.

'Neidhöhle' is 'cavern of greed'.

		Drum schnell! Schaffe das Schwert,
Adventure		in der Welt will ich es *schwing*en.

MIME

Adventure Das Schwert? O Not!

SIEGFRIED

Adventure⌉ Rasch in die Schmiede!
        Weis, was du schufst!

MIME

Adventure   *Forge*⌉ Verfluchter Stahl!
        Zu flicken versteh ich ihn nicht:
        den zähen Zauber
        bezwingt keines Zwergen Kraft.
        Wer das Fürchten nicht kennt,
        der fänd wohl eher die Kunst.

SIEGFRIED

Forge⌉ Feine Finten
      weiss mir der Faule;
Adventure dass er ein *Stümp*er,
      sollt er gestehn:
Forge nun *lügt* er sich listig heraus!
      Her mit den Stücken,
Sword fort mit dem *Stümp*er!
      Des Vaters Stahl
      fügt sich wohl mir:
Horn Call ich selbst schweisse das *Schwert*!

MIME

Horn Call⌉ Hättest du fleissig
Forge die Kunst ge*pflegt*,
      jetzt käm dir's wahrlich zugut:
      doch lässig warst du
Forge stets in der *Lehr*:
      was willst du Rechtes nun rüsten?

SIEGFRIED

Horn Call⌉ Was der Meister nicht kann,
Forge vermöcht es der *Knabe*,
      hätt er ihm immer gehorcht?
      Jetzt mach dich fort,
      misch dich nicht drein:
      sonst fällst du mir mit ins Feuer!

Make haste! Forge me the sword!
In the world – there shall I wield it.

MIME
The sword? The sword?

SIEGFRIED
Into the smithy!
Show me your skill!

MIME
Accursed steel!
It cannot be mended again.
Its stubborn magic
defeats all my dwarfish skill.
One who does not know fear,
is far less likely to fail.

SIEGFRIED
With his wiles
the trickster would trap me.
He is a bungler:
he should admit,
and not try to lie his way out.
Fetch me the fragments!
Off with the botcher!
My father's steel
yields to the son,
and he shall forge it himself.
[flinging Mime's tools about, he sets to
work]

MIME
If you had only
acquired the craft,
you now would know what to do.
But you were always
lazy to learn.
How will you now set about it?

SIEGFRIED
When the teacher has failed,
what hope for the pupil,
had he obeyed and observed?
Out of my way,
meddle no more,
or else you'll fall in the fire!

Siegmund, Siegfried's father,
gained his sword by plucking it
from Hunding's tree. The son
faces an even harder task – he
has to reforge the splinters.

MIME

Horn Call
Was machst du denn da?
Nimm doch die Löte:
den Brei braut ich schon längst.

SIEGFRIED

Horn Call
Fort mit dem Brei!
Ich brauch ihn nicht:
mit Bappe back ich kein Schwert!

MIME

Horn Call
Du zerfeilst die Feile,
zerreibst die Raspel:
wie willst du den Stahl
    zerstampfen?

SIEGFRIED

Horn Call
Zersponnen muss ich
in Späne ihn sehn:
was entzwei ist, zwing ich mir so.

MIME

Horn Call
Hier hilft kein Kluger,
das seh ich klar:
hier hilft dem Dummen
die Dummheit allein!
Wie er sich rührt
und mächtig regt!
Ihm schwindet der Stahl,
Loge
doch wird ihm nicht *schwül*!

Nun ward ich so alt
wie Höhl' und Wald
und hab nicht so was gesehn!

Mit dem Schwert gelingt's,
das lern ich wohl:
Shuffle
furchtlos fegt er's zu *ganz.*
Loge
Der Wandrer wusst es gut!
Wie berg ich nun
mein banges Haupt?
Siegfried
Dem *kühn*en Knaben verfiel's,

[He heaps a large pile of charcoal on the
hearth and blows the fire, while he fixes
the fragments of the sword in a vice.
He then files them to shreds. Mime watches
him.]

MIME
Now heaven forbid!
Here, take the solder!
I made the mixture myself.

SIEGFRIED
Off with the brew!
No need for that:
a sword is not fashioned with filth!

MIME
But the file you've fumbled,
the rasp you've ruined;
you're pounding the steel to pieces!

SIEGFRIED
It must be pounded
and shivered to shreds.
What is broken shall be restored.

MIME
My skill's no help here,
that much I see.
The fool is helped
by his folly alone.
Look how he toils
and moves with might.
The steel is in shreds,
but he's not yet done.
[Siegfried fans the fire to its brightest glow]
I'm old and I'm grave
as copse and cave,
I've never seen such a sight!
[Mime seats himself further away, while
Siegfried continues his impetuous filing]
He will win that sword,
I can see it now,
fearless, filing away.
How right the Wanderer was!
What help is there
for Mime's head?
The boy will chisel it off!

The woodwind break into trills,
emphasizing Siegfried's *joie de
vivre*.

Mime's rhyming couplet, 'I'm old
and I'm grave as copse and cave',
has a fairy tale ring. Indeed, in
Grimm's 'Wichtelmänner' (The
Elves), Wagner found: 'Nun bin
ich so alt wie der Westerwald'
('now I am as old as the Westerwald').

Horn Call	*(Loge)*	lehrt ihn nicht Fafner die *Furcht*!
Dragon		Doch weh mir Armen!
		Wie würgt' er den Wurm,
		erführ er das Fürchten von ihm?
	Ring	Wie erräng er mir den *Ring*?
		Verfluchte Klemme!
		Da klebt ich fest,
		fänd ich nicht klugen Rat,
		wie den Furchtlosen selbst ich
		bezwäng.

SIEGFRIED

		He, Mime! Geschwind!
		Wie heisst das Schwert,
	Sword	das ich in Späne *zer*sponnen?

MIME

Nothung		*Noth*ung nennt sich
		das neidliche Schwert:
Horn Call		deine Mutter gab mir die *Mär*.

SIEGFRIED

Nothung		*Noth*ung! Nothung!
		Neidliches Schwert!
Action		Was musstest du zerspringen?
		Zu Spreu nun schuf ich
		die scharfe Pracht,
Horn Call		im Tiegel brat ich die *Spä*ne.
		Hoho! Hoho!
		Hohei! Hohei! Hoho!
		Blase, Balg!
Action		Blase die Glut!
		Wild im Walde
		wuchs ein Baum,
		den hab ich im Forst gefällt:
		die braune Esche
		brannt ich zur Kohl',
Horn Call		auf dem Herd nun liegt sie gehäuft.
		Hoho! Hoho!
		Hohei! Hohei! Hoho!
		Blase, Balg!
Action		Blase die Glut!
		Des Baumes Kohle,
		wie brennt sie kühn;
		wie glüht sie hell und hehr!

Fafner must fill him with fear!
But that's no good, either!
The dragon is safe,
as soon as he teaches him fear:
then the ring is out of my reach.
Accurst dilemma!
I'll come off worst,
unless I find a way
how to foil the fearless boy.

In the *Thidrek Saga*, one of Wagner's chief sources, the smith Welent also reforges a splintered sword, adding a secret ingredient to the pulp – bird dropping. Wagner fought shy. Anyway, he needed an immaculate bird for the next act.

SIEGFRIED [having filed down the pieces, he puts them in a crucible which he places on the hearth fire]
Quick, Mime, what is
the name of the sword
that I have pounded to pieces?

MIME
Nothung, that is
the glorious sword,
and your mother gave me its name.

Wagner originally planned to make Siegfried forge the sword 'under Mime's supervision'. He soon knew better.

SIEGFRIED [during the following he blows the fire with the bellows]
Nothung! Nothung!
Glorious sword!
Why did you have to shatter?
I chopped to chaff now
your sharp-edged pride;
the pot shall melt all the pieces.
Hoho! Hoho!
Hohei! Hohei! Hoho!
Bellows, blow!
Blow the glow!
Wild in woodlands
grew a tree;
I cut it there in the copse.
The brown-hued ash
to charcoal I burned;
now it lies in heaps on the hearth.
Hoho! Hoho!
Hohei! Hohei! Hoho!
Bellows, blow!
Blow the glow!
The cinders burn
so bravely now;
their blush is bright and bold.

We are in D minor, Wagner's 'storm' key, used so effectively in *Walküre* in the prelude to Act I and at the end of Act II, at the end of Act II of *Tristan* and in the prelude to *Der fliegende Holländer*. Here, the key indicates the turmoil in Siegfried's heart.

A perfect tone-painting: the hammer swings upwards then comes crashing down, while mighty sparks are flying.

(Action) | In springenden Funken
sprühet sie auf:
Hohei! Hoho! Hohei!
Horn Call | zerschmilzt mir des Stahles *Spreu.*
Hoho! Hoho!
Hohei! Hohei! Hoho!
Blase, Balg!
Blase die Glut!

MIME
Er schmiedet das Schwert
und Fafner fällt er:
das seh ich nun deutlich voraus.
Hort und Ring
Ring | erringt er im Harst:
Forge | wie erwerb ich mir den Gewinn?
Mit Witz und List
gewinn ich beides
und berge heil mein Haupt.

SIEGFRIED
Hoho! Hoho!
Dragon | Hohei! Hohei! Hohei!

MIME
Rang er sich müd mit dem Wurm,
Oblivion | von der Müh erlab ihn ein *Trunk*:

aus würzgen Säften,
die ich gesammelt,
brau ich den Trank für ihn:
wenig Tropfen nur
braucht er zu trinken,
Sword | sinnlos sinkt er in Schlaf.
Mit der eignen Waffe,
die er sich gewonnen,
räum ich ihn leicht aus dem Weg,
erlange mir Ring und Hort.
Hei! Weiser Wandrer!
Dünkt ich dich dumm?
Forge | Wie gefällt dir *nun*
mein feiner Witz?
Fand ich mir wohl
Sword | Rat und Ruh?

SIEGFRIED
Nothung | *Noth*ung! Nothung!
Neidliches Schwert!
Action | Nun schmolz deines Stahles *Spreu*!

The showering sparks
are leaping up high:
Hohei! Hoho! Hohei!
Now melt me the friable steel!
Hoho! Hoho!
Hohei! Hohei! Hoho!
Bellows, blow!
Blow the glow!

MIME [sitting apart, to himself]
He fashions the sword,
and Fafner founders:
that's easy enough to foresee.
Hoard and ring
will then fall to him;
but how can I gather the gains?
With craft and wit
they must be captured,
and I shall save my head.

SIEGFRIED
Hoho! Hoho!
Hohei! Hohei! Hohei!

MIME
When he has butchered the beast,
I will quench his thirst with a
    drink.
From deadly spices
that I have stored,
I'll brew him a dainty draught.
Let him taste but one drop
of the stuff,
and soft shall then be his sleep.
With the selfsame sword
that now he is forging,
he shall be sent to his doom,   Siegfried kills the dragon; Mime
and mine will be ring and gold!   kills Siegfried. Has the dwarf has
So, my wise wanderer,   solved his problem?
who is the fool?
Are you pleased with me
and with my plot?
Have I procured
lasting peace?

SIEGFRIED   The smelting is accomplished; so
Nothung! Nothung!   is the Smelting Song. Now for the
Glorious sword!   forging and Siegfried's Forging
Now melts the shredded steel.   Song.

(Action) Im eignen Schweisse
schwimmst du nun.

Bald schwing ich dich als mein
   Schwert!
In das Wasser floss
ein Feuerfluss:
grimmiger Zorn
zischt' ihm da auf!
Wie sehrend er floss,
in des Wassers Flut
fliesst er nicht mehr.
Starr ward er und steif,
herrisch der harte Stahl:

Sword heisses *Blut* doch
Action fliesst ihm *bald*!
Nun schwitze noch einmal,
Horn Call dass ich dich schweisse,
Nothung *Noth*ung, neidliches Schwert!

Was schafft der Tölpel
dort mit dem Topf?
Brenn ich hier Stahl,
braust du dort Sudel?

MIME
Zuschanden kam ein Schmied;
den Lehrer sein Knabe lehrt:
mit der Kunst nun ist's beim
   Alten aus,
als Koch dient er dem Kind.
Brennt er das Eisen zu Brei,
aus Eiern braut
der Alte ihm Sud.

SIEGFRIED
Mime, der Künstler,
Forge lernt jetzt *koch*en;
das Schmieden schmeckt ihm
   nicht mehr.
Seine Schwerter alle
hab ich zerschmissen;
Action was er kocht, ich kost es ihm nicht!

In your own sweat
you're swimming now.
[he pours the contents of the crucible into a
mould, then plunges the mould into a pail of
water, accompanied by much steam and
hissing]
I soon shall swing my own
    sword!
In the water flowed
a flood of fire;
searing, hot hate
hissed from the blade.
How fiercely it flowed
in the cooling flood;
now it shall rest.
Strong is it and stiff,
lordly the stubborn steel.
[he thrusts the steel into the fire and
vigorously works the bellows]
Blood shall soon gush
from the blade.
Now sweat once again,
so that I may shape you,
Nothung, glorious sword!
[he watches Mime, who busies himself, in
high spirits, with his cooking utensils]
What does the bungler there
with his pot?
I'm burning steel –
what are you brewing?

MIME
A smith I am no more.
The master must learn from you.
I'm a poor old dwarf whose skill
    has gone.
As cook I'll serve the boy.
You make a soup of the steel,
with eggs I brew
a bonny, brave broth.

SIEGFRIED
Mime the master
takes up cooking;
he's lost his taste for the
    forge.
All the swords that he made,
I have shattered to pieces.
What he cooks, I care not to taste.

A vehement sequence of pulsat-
ing chords accompanies both
Siegfried's forging and Mime's
brewing. While Siegfried's chords
are openly diatonic, Mime's are
deviously chromatic.

Das Fürchten zu lernen,
will er mich führen;
ein Ferner soll es mich lehren:

was am besten er kann,
mir bringt er's nicht bei:
als Stümper besteht er in allem!

Hoho! Hoho! Hahei!
Schmiede, mein Hammer,
ein hartes Schwert!
Hoho! Hahei!
Hoho! Hahei!
Einst färbte Blut
dein falbes Blau;
sein rotes Rieseln
rötete dich:
kalt lachtest du da,
das warme lecktest du kühl!
Heiaho! Haha!
Haheiaha!
Nun hat die Glut
dich rot geglüht;
deine weiche Härte
dem Hammer weicht:
zornig sprühst du mir Funken,
dass ich dich Spröden gezähmt!
Heiaho! Heiaho!
Heiahohoho!

Sword   Ha*hei*!

MIME
Er schafft sich ein scharfes
  Schwert,
Fafner zu fällen,
der Zwerge Feind:
ich braut' ein Truggetränk,
Siegfried zu fangen,
dem Fafner fiel.
Gelingen muss mir die List;
lachen muss mir der Lohn!

SIEGFRIED
Hoho! Hoho!
Hahei!

[he draws the mould from the fire, breaks it,
and places the glowing steel on the anvil]
To show me what fear is,
that he has promised.
Some far-off master should teach
    me,
for all Mime can teach,
is a waste of my time.
A fool I have found him in all
    things.
Hoho! Hoho! Hohei!
Forge me, my hammer,
a hardy sword!
Hoho! Hahei!
Hoho! Hahei!
Blood-stained was once
your steely blue,
and crimson ripples
reddened the blade.
Cold laughter was yours;
you cooled the blood on the blade.
Heiaho! Haha!
Haheiaha!
With fiery flame
you now are flushed,
as the softened steel
to the hammer yields.
Angry sparks you are spouting,
for I have harnessed your pride.
Heiaho! Heiaho!
Heiahohoho!
Hahei!

MIME
He's shaping the sharpest
    sword.
Fafner will feel it,
the Niblungs' foe.
A deadly drink I've brewed.
Siegfried must perish,
when Fafner falls.
My wits must win me that catch!
Fortune smiles on the brave.
[he pours the contents of the pot into a flask]

SIEGFRIED
Hoho! Hoho!
Hahei!

Schmiede, mein Hammer,
ein hartes Schwert!
Hoho! Hahei!
Hahei! Hoho!
Der frohen Funken
wie freu ich mich;
es ziert den Kühnen
des Zornes Kraft:
lustig lachst du mich an,
stellst du auch grimm dich und
   gram!
Heiaho! Haha!
Haheiaha!
Durch Glut und Hammer
glückt' es mir;
mit starken Schlägen
streck ich dich:
nun schwinde die rote Scham;

werde kalt und hart, wie du kannst.
Heiaho! Heiaho!
Heiahohoho!
Heia!

MIME
Forge Den der *Bru*der schuf,
Shuffle den schimmernden Reif,
in den er gezaubert
zwingende Kraft,
das helle Gold,
das zum Herrscher macht,
ihn hab ich gewonnen!
Forge Ich walte sein!
Shuffle *Al*berich selbst,
der einst mich band,
zur Zwergenfrone
zwing ich ihn nun;
als Niblungenfürst
fahr ich danieder;
gehorchen soll mir
Forge alles *Heer*!
Der verachtete Zwerg,
wie wird er geehrt!
Zu dem Horte hin drängt sich
Gott und Held:
vor meinem Nicken
neigt sich die Welt,
vor meinem Zorne

Forge me, my hammer,
a hardy sword!
Hoho! Hahei!
Hahei! Hoho!
The dazzling sparks
delight my eyes.
Brave blade, rejoice
in your wrathful rage.
Look and laugh at your lord,
though you seem grisly and
   grim!
Heiaho! Haha!
Haheiaha!
The heat and hammer
brought me luck;
with blazing blows
I stretched you straight.
Now shake off your blush of
   shame,
and be cold, be hard, be yourself!
Heiaho! Heiaho!
Heiahohoho!
Heia! [he plunges the sword into
the water]

MIME
Once my brother wrought
a shimmering ring,
and on it he laid
a lasting spell.
That gleaming gold
gives surpassing power:
that power is mine now;
I've paid the price!
Alberich, he
who made me a slave,
in dwarfish thrall
he soon shall be thrust.
As Nibelheim's prince
they all shall worship
and serve me ever,
man for man!
The contemptible dwarf,
revered shall he be!
To the hoard they will hasten,
gods and men.
At Mime's bidding
all shall bow down,
and all shall bend their knee,

The part of Siegfried requires a
muscular musician who is able to
vary the intensity of his hammer
blows. Wagner directs: '/\ for a
very strong blow, \/ for a lighter
blow and | for a very light blow.'

Siegfried's jubilant shout 'Heiaho'
is not easy to sing in tune. The
notes fall from top A, via F, to B.
At the Bayreuth rehearsals the
composer directed his Siegfried
not to *sing* but to *yodel* those
notes.

Siegfried plunges the sword into
the water-trough, and the orchestra plummets down in sympathy.

zittert sie hin!
Dann wahrlich müht sich

Forge Mime nicht *mehr*:
ihm schaffen andre
den ewgen Schatz.

Forge Mime, der *kühn*e,
Mime ist König,
Fürst der Alben,
Walter des Alls!
Hei, Mime! Wie glückte dir das!
Wer hätte wohl das gedacht?

SIEGFRIED

Nothung *Noth*ung! Nothung!
Neidliches Schwert!
Jetzt haftest du wieder im
    Heft.
Warst du entzwei,
ich zwang dich zu ganz;
kein Schlag soll nun dich mehr zer
    schlagen.
Dem sterbenden Vater
zersprang der Stahl,
der lebende Sohn
schuf ihn neu:
nun lacht ihm sein heller Schein,
seine Schärfe schneidet ihm hart.

Nothung *Noth*ung! Nothung!
Sword Neidliches *Schwert*!
Zum Leben weckt ich dich wieder.
Tot lagst du
in Trümmern dort,
jetzt leuchtest du trotzig und hehr.
Zeige den Schächern
nun deinen Schein!
Schlage den Falschen,
fälle den Schelm!

Horn Call *Schau*, Mime, du Schmied:

Sword so schneidet Siegfrieds *Schwert*!

when I frown.
No longer will I
struggle and sweat.
Others shall win me
unending wealth.
Mime the mighty!
Mime the monarch!
Niblung ruler!
Lord of the world!
Hei, Mime! You fortunate man!
What luck equals Mime's luck?

SIEGFRIED
Nothung! Nothung!
Glorious sword!
Once more you are held in your
    hilt.
Sundered no more:
I forged you anew.
No second stroke shall ever split
    you!
My father was doomed,
when you came undone;
his living son
forged you anew.
For me now you laugh aloud;
you shall joust with joy evermore!
Nothung! Nothung!
Glorious sword!
To life again I awoke you.
Dead were you,
in shattered shreds,
now gleaming defiant and fair.
Let all offenders
witness your worth!
Cut down all rascals,
cut down all rogues!
See, Mime, you smith:
[he raises the sword]
keen-edged is Siegfried's sword!
[He splits the anvil with one stroke. Mime,
who has jumped on to a stool in his
ecstasy, now falls down to the ground, while
Siegfried holds his sword aloft.]

Siegfried greets his newly forged
sword Nothung with a brief but
intense hymn of praise, creating
an almost comical contrast with
Mime's fidgety dream of revenge.

Against Siegfried's top A on the
Nothung motif, the full orchestra,
fortissimo, hallows the momentous deed with a solo trumpet
celebrating the sword.

The act ends with Siegfried holding his sword aloft. This parallels
the end of the first act of
Walküre, where Siegfried's father
brandished his sword with a like
gesture.

The highly dramatic ending, with
Nothung splitting the anvil, owes
much to the *Thidrek Saga*, where
Sigurd (Siegfried) learns to use
the hammer, and with his first
blow shatters Mime's anvil. Mime
is not amused and states, 'You
will never become a decent
smith.'

Much Ado about Fear

'The Tale of the Youth who Set Out to Learn Fear' is the title of one of Grimm's *Fairy Tales*, well known to Wagner. What did it have to offer to the poet and composer of the *Ring*?

'People always say, something gives them the creeps. Nothing gives me the creeps. It must be a skill which I have not mastered.' Thus Grimm's fearless lad. 'Is it a skill, why am I unskilled? Come on and teach me what fear is!' Thus Siegfried to Mime.

While trying to acquire the elusive skill, Grimm's lad meets a carter who asks him his name. 'I don't know,' he replies. 'Where are you from?' 'I don't know.' 'Who is your father?' 'I'm not allowed to tell you.' Effortlessly the fairy tale jumps from *Siegfried* to *Parsifal*. The tale then mentions the king's beautiful daughter whom the youth is to marry, a vast treasure, horrible creatures with enormous, sharp claws, which the lad kills, and an anvil which he splits with one single blow.

No wonder that Wagner wrote to his friend Uhlig, in May 1851, 'Did I not write to you, some time ago, about a light-hearted subject? It concerned the lad who set out to discover what fear is, but is too slow-witted to learn it. Imagine my shock, when I suddenly realized that this lad is none other than my Young Siegfried who wins the hoard and wakes Brünnhilde!'

Indeed, three years before Wagner started to write the first prose sketch of *Der junge Siegfried*, he told his sculptor friend Gustav Adolph Kietz, 'I shall write no more operas, but fairy tales, like the one about the lad who does not know fear.' Clearly, the topic haunted him.

Let us take a closer look at the verse draft *Der junge Siegfried* (later just *Siegfried*), written in 1851. In the draft Mime attempts to teach Siegfried fear before – not after – the dialogue with the Wanderer. He informs Siegfried, blithely bearing false witness:

MIME
Hear, what your mother
confided to me!
Mime, she said,
you wise man –
once my child has grown up,
protect the bold fellow in the forest!

The world is treacherous and false;
it sets traps for simple souls.
Only he who has learnt fear,
has a chance to survive.

SIEGFRIED
And my mother has told you that?

MIME
Trust me, those are her very words!

SIEGFRIED
I would like to learn fear!

Only in the final version of the poem of *Siegfried* shall we meet
Wagner's final thoughts on the issue of fear:

Act I, scene 3:
Mime hypnotizes himself into a state of utter terror.

Act I, scene 3:
Mime tries to teach Siegfried fear.

Act II, scene 2:
Fafner fails to teach Siegfried fear.

Act III, scene 3:
Siegfried learns fear from Brünnhilde: 'A woman folded in
sleep has taught me the meaning of fear.'

Act III, scene 3:
Brünnhilde learns fear from Siegfried: 'O Siegfried, pity my
fear!'

Act III, scene 3:
Siegfried unlearns fear: 'I fear I forgot how to fear.'

Concluding Observations

1. When Tolstoy saw *Siegfried* at Bayreuth, he observed: 'An actor in tight-fitting breeches was seated before an object that was meant to represent an anvil. He wore a wig and false beard; his white and manicured hands had nothing of the workman about them; and his easy air, prominent belly, and flabby muscles readily betrayed the actor. With an absurd hammer he struck – as no one else would ever strike – a fantastic-looking sword blade. One guessed he was a dwarf because when he walked he bent his legs at the knees. He cried out a great deal and opened his mouth in a queer fashion ... It was all so artificial and stupid that I had great difficulty in sitting it out.'

2. When Wieland Wagner, the composer's grandson, produced the *Ring* at Bayreuth, he observed: 'Of course I can make Mime a dainty dwarf. That will look quite attractive, rather like the witch in *Hänsel and Gretel* ... But Mime is far more than that. He is a dangerous megalomaniac well armed with a whole arsenal of vile tricks. All that I must present on the stage.'

3. Siegfried can be observed as a typical fairy-tale hero. The unwritten law of the fairy tale allows the unexpected and the impossible. Thus Siegfried can forge a sword by intuition. He can understand the language of bird and dragon. He can walk, unscathed, through a wall of flames. He can topple a god.

4. The action of Act I can be observed as a gigantic U-turn:

Mime tries to forge a sword	Siegfried succeeds in forging a sword
Siegfried in high spirits	Siegfried in high spirits
Siegfried and Mime	Siegfried and Mime
Siegfried demands his sword	Siegfried demands his sword
Mime's despair	Mime's despair

The Wanderer and Mime

5. In a letter to Julie Ritter of May 1857 Wagner made the following erroneous observation: 'I am sure my *Siegfried* will become my most popular work and will spread quickly and successfully. Thus, *Siegfried* will become the founder of a whole Nibelungen dynasty by preparing the way for the other dramas.'

He was wrong. It was *Walküre* that prepared the way for the rest of the tetralogy. *Siegfried*, for some unfathomable reason, remains the least popular section of the *Ring*.

Do audiences become impatient with all-male voices for two whole acts (not counting the female voice of the Woodbird)? Do they miss those stage spectaculars of the other *Ring* dramas (a rainbow bridge, flying horses) – or their weird and wonderful locales (subterranean goldmines, a castle in the sky)? Or perhaps the intrusion of the supernatural?

Audiences surely undervalue the quiet but stirring serenity of Act II's forest scene, and the heady beauties of the final love scene. And yet, the comic aspects and tranquillities of *Siegfried*, the third opera of the tetralogy, are surely meant to make us palpitate at the terror of the fourth, *Götterdämmerung*.

6. We observe a new generation growing up. Will these humans, Siegfried, Brünnhilde and Hagen (the son that will be born to Alberich), be able to run the world more humanely, more ethically than the old, storm-tossed eternals?

Siegfried kills the dragon: 'Nothung
sticks in your gizzard!'

II

Act

Synopsis
Leitmotifs
Libretto

Act II: Story

The Depth of the Forest

Scene 1
Alberich is keeping watch near the entrance to Fafner's cave. Wotan arrives, again as the Wanderer, and acquaints Alberich with Mime's designs on the ring. He wakes Fafner, so that Alberich may ask the monster to grant him the ring in exchange for being warned of Siegfried's approach. Fafner declines, and the Wanderer disappears, laughing.

Scene 2
Mime arrives with Siegfried. The dwarf tries, once again, to teach the lad fear, by describing the monster's fearsome aspect and habits. Siegfried, still unafraid, decides to pit his wits and his strength against the dragon, and sends Mime away. He reclines in the shade of a tree and listens to the birds above him. He muses about his dead parents. Trying to imitate the song of one of the birds, he fashions a reed pipe. Its sound fails to establish the desired contact, but when he blows his horn, the dragon (Fafner) comes out of his lair. Siegfried pierces the heart of the monster, who, with his dying breath, warns Siegfried that Mime intends to kill him. Licking the dragon's blood off his fingers causes Siegfried to understand the language of the birds. One of them advises him to take possession of the ring and the Tarnhelm.

Scene 3
While Siegfried is inside the monster's cave, Mime is intercepted by Alberich. Both brothers claim to be legitimate heirs to Fafner's hoard. Siegfried emerges, holding both Tarnhelm and ring, while Alberich and Mime hide and watch. The Woodbird warns Siegfried to beware of Mime, who now comes out of his hiding place and offers Siegfried a drink. As a consequence of having tasted the dragon's blood, Siegfried not only understands the birds' language, but also Mime's treacherous thoughts: Mime intends to poison Siegfried, in order to gain ring, Tarnhelm and the golden treasure. To prevent this, Siegfried kills him. The bird now advises him to make his way through the wall of fire which surrounds the slumbering Brünnhilde (the destined bride of the fearless Siegfried). The bird flutters ahead, and Siegfried follows.

Mime and Alberich quarrel
over Fafner's hoard; illustration
by Arthur Rackham (1911)

Act II: Action

Siegfried in the forest;
illustration by Franz Stassen
(1914)

Act II: Leitmotifs

The leitmotifs new to the act follow in chronological order, together with the page number of first appearance.

Fafner   p.100

This grisly motif consists of two sections. The first, played by the double basses, sweeps upwards, from G flat to C, an augmented fourth; it is closely related to the Nibelungen Hate motif, which also sweeps upwards, but only by the interval of a perfect fourth. The second section is played by two kettledrums, one tuned to C, the other to F sharp, enharmonically identical to the augmented fourth of the first section. Augmented and diminished intervals lack the unambiguity of perfect, major and minor intervals. Their indeterminate aspect, when reinforced by the kettledrum's sombre sound, fits the motif to perfection. Is Fafner still himself? Is his transformation into a monster permanent or temporary? Has he repented of the murder of his brother Fasolt? Is he atoning for his brutish past by guarding the ring, which can do no mischief while he sleeps upon it?

Woodbird   p.120

The motif is based on the pentatonic scale, giving it an air of carefree buoyancy. The pentatonic scale is much in evidence in old Celtic and Scottish folk songs, as well as in Far Eastern music. In the forest scene in *Siegfried* the motif appears in four different shapes – the three others are shown below.

Fafner Dragon Brooding Ring
Fafner Curse Fafner
Curse Nibelungen Hate Ring
Grief Ring Fafner

II. Akt: 1. Szene

Vorspiel

Nibelungen Hate ⌉ **ALBERICH**
In Wald und Nacht
vor Neidhöhl' halt ich Wacht;
es lauscht mein Ohr,
mühvoll lugt mein Aug'.
Banger Tag,
Ride⌉ Authority⌉ bebst du schon auf?
Dämmerst du dort
durch das Dunkel her?

Welcher Glanz glitzert dort auf?

Näher schimmert
ein heller Schein;
es rennt wie ein leuchtendes Ross,
bricht durch den Wald
brausend daher.
Naht schon des Wurmes Würger?
Curse Ist's schon, der Fafner fällt?

Fafner Das Licht erlischt
der Glanz barg sich dem Blick;
Curse Nibelungen Hate Nacht *ist's wieder.*
Wer naht dort schimmernd im
Schatten?

WANDERER
Zur Neidhöhle
fuhr ich bei Nacht:
Walhall wen gewahr ich im Dunkel dort?

ALBERICH
Du selbst lässt dich hier sehn?
Was willst du hier?

Act II: Scene 1

Prelude

[Deep in the Forest. Entrance to a cavern. Night.]

ALBERICH
This dusky wood
by Neidhöhl is my haunt.
My ears keep watch,
keenly peer my eyes.
Day of doom,
is this your dawn?
What is it, breaks
through the blackness there?
[a stormwind comes from the forest]
What is that glow glimmering
    bright?
Nearer and nearer –
it shines on me,
it speeds like a fiery steed,
storms through the wood,
rushing at me.
Is it the dragon-slayer?
Is this the dragon's doom?
[the wind dies down]
The light has gone,
the glow glimmers no more.
All is darkness.
What shimmers there, in the shadow?

WANDERER
To Neidhöhl
by night have I come.
Who is hid in the darkness there?
[sudden moonlight reveals the Wanderer's
face]

ALBERICH [recoils, then starts furiously]
Yourself? Really yourself?
What would you here?

'Neidhöhl' is 'cavern of greed',
hence Fafner's cave. Wagner
derived the name from 'Gnita-
heide' ('heath of envy'), as named
in his old Germanic sources.

The prelude conjures up a snake-
pit of gloom, poison and lovelessness. Two kettledrums, tuned C
and F sharp, intone the Fafner
motif. The interval is the augmented fourth, or 'diabolus in
musica'; it derives from the plain
and honest interval of a fourth
which formed the old Giants
motif. But Fafner is no longer a
plain and not-so-honest giant; he
is a diabolic monster, guarding his
ill-gotten treasure by sleeping
upon it. After the sixth Fafner
motif, a ponderous contrabass
tuba growls a snaky ascending
theme which seems to represent
the powers of darkness.

The Ride and Authority motifs
announce Wotan's approach.

Fort, aus dem Weg!
Von dannen, schamloser Dieb!

WANDERER
Schwarz-Alberich,
schweifst du hier?
Hütest du Fafners Haus?

ALBERICH
Jagst du auf neue
Neidtat umher?
Weile nicht hier!
Weiche von hinnen!
Genug des Truges

Siegfried *tränk*te die Stätte mit Not.

Drum, du Frecher,
lass sie jetzt frei!

Wanderer **WANDERER**
Zu schauen kam ich,
nicht zu schaffen:
wer wehrte mir Wandrers Fahrt?

ALBERICH
Du Rat wütender Ränke!
Wär ich dir zu lieb
doch noch dumm wie damals,
als du mich Blöden bandest!
Wie leicht geriet es,

Wotan's Frustration den Ring mir nochmals zu rauben!

Hab Acht: deine Kunst
kenne ich wohl;
doch wo du schwach bist,
blieb mir auch nicht verschwiegen.
Mit meinen Schätzen
zahltest du Schulden;
mein Ring lohnte

Walhall der Riesen *Müh'*,
Treaty die deine Burg dir ge*baut*.
Was mit den Trotz'gen
einst du vertragen,
dess Runen wahrt noch heut

Troth deines Speeres herrischer *Schaft*.
Nicht du darfst,
was als Zoll du gezahlt,
den Riesen wieder entreissen:
du selbst zerspelltest

Out of my sight!
Go elsewhere, infamous thief!

WANDERER
Black-Alberich,
hiding here?
Haunting old Fafner's house?

ALBERICH
Ever intent on
havoc and harm?
Be on your way!
Off! Do not linger!
Too much deception
drenches the earth with your
    tricks.
So, you villain,
spare us more spite!

WANDERER
I came to look,
but not to labour.
Who bars the Wanderer's way?

ALBERICH
You false, pitiless plotter!
You would have me dull,
as you once had found me,
when I became your captive.
If I would let you,
once more my ring you would
    covet.
Beware, for your wiles
I know too well;
also your weakness
is no longer a secret.
My stolen treasure,
ransomed your Freia.
My ring paid
for the giants' pains
who built your castle up high.
With those rude brutes
you made a bad bargain,
whose runes can still be seen
on the arrogant shaft of your spear.
This binds you.
For the wages you paid,
you dare not pluck from the giants.
You'd lose forever

Wotan continues to play the role
he assumed in the first act, that
of a non-participating observer.
This mental detachment is to be
severely tested in the next act,
when he encounters Siegfried.

Here Alberich represents Wotan's
conscience.

deines Speeres Schaft:
in deiner Hand
der herrische Stab,

Fafner   *Arrogance*   der *starke* zerstiebte wie *Spreu.*
Wanderer

WANDERER
Durch Vertrages Treue-Runen
band er dich

Treaty   Bösen mir nicht:
dich beugt er mir durch seine
    Kraft:
zum Krieg drum wahr ich ihn

Nibelungen Hate   *wohl.*

ALBERICH
Wie stolz du dräust
in trotziger Stärke,
und wie dir's im Busen doch

Curse   bangt!
Verfallen dem Tod
durch meinen Fluch

Nibelungen Hate   ist des Hortes Hüter:
wer – wird ihn beerben?
Wird der neidliche Hort

Nibelungen Hate   dem Niblung wieder gehören?
Das sehrt dich mit ew'ger Sorge!
Denn fass ich ihn wieder
einst in der Faust,
anders als dumme Riesen

Ring   *üb'* ich des Ringes Kraft:
dann zittre der Helden

Grief   heiliger Hüter!
Walhalls Höhen
stürm ich mit Hellas Heer:

Arrogance   der Welt walte dann *ich!*

WANDERER
Deinen Sinn kenn ich;
doch sorgt er mich nicht;
des Ringes waltet

Wotan's Frustration   wer ihn gewinnt.

ALBERICH
Wie dunkel sprichst du,

Sword   was ich deutlich doch *weiss!*
An Heldensöhne
hält dich dein Trotz,

Liebe-Tragik   die traut deinem *Blu*te entblüht.
Pflegtest du wohl eines Knaben,

your great spear's control.
In your own hand
that swaggering staff
would shamefully shiver to bits.

WANDERER
By the runes of trusted treaties,
you are no
creature of mine.
My spear restrains you by its
    strength.
It brings me victory in war.

ALBERICH
You brag, you boast,
you bluster so boldly,
and yet, how you fear your own
    fate!
Grim death is decreed,
by Alberich's curse,
for the treasure's guardian.
But who shall inherit?
Will the precious hoard
to the Niblung again be allotted?
That causes you keen vexation.
For once I have gripped it
with my own fist,
better than blundering giants
shall I control that ring.
Then tremble, you god,
you guardian of heroes!
Walhall's towers
crumble to Hella's host.
Behold, mine is the world!

Alberich repeats his threat, first uttered in *Rheingold*, of annihilating Walhall and all the gods.

Hella is the underworld.

WANDERER
Though I know your design,
it troubles me not.
The ring's true owner
shall seize the ring.

ALBERICH
You speak in riddles,
but I know what I know.
On heroes' offspring
you pin your hope –
some hero begot by your blood.
Have you not fostered a fellow,

In his prose draft of *Der junge Siegfried* Wagner allots a very lengthy reiteration of past events to Alberich. He later dropped this in favour of composing *Rheingold*, where those events could be shown rather than reported.

der klug die Frucht dir pflücke,
Wotan's Frustration   die du – nicht brechen darfst!

WANDERER
Mit mir nicht,
hadre mit Mime:
dein Bruder bringt dir Gefahr;
einen Knaben führt er daher,
der Fafner ihm fällen soll.
Nichts weiss der von mir;
der Niblung nützt ihn für sich.
Drum sag ich dir, Gesell:
Brooding   tue frei, wie dir's frommt!
Höre mich wohl,
sei auf der Hut;
nicht kennt der Knabe den Ring,
Treaty   doch Mime kundet' ihn aus.

ALBERICH
Deine Hand hieltest du vom Hort?

WANDERER
Wen ich liebe,
lass ich für sich gewähren;
Freedom   er *steh* oder fall',
sein Herr ist er:
Helden nur können mir frommen.

ALBERICH
Mit Mime räng ich
allein um den Ring?

WANDERER
Ausser dir begehrt er
einzig das Gold.

ALBERICH
Und dennoch gewänn ich ihn nicht?

WANDERER
Ein Helde naht,
den Hort zu befrein;
Dragon   zwei Niblungen geizen das *Gold*:
Fafner fällt,
der den Ring bewacht:
wer ihn rafft, hat ihn gewonnen.
Willst du noch mehr?
Fafner   Dort liegt der Wurm:

that one day he might plunder
the fruit you dare not pluck?

WANDERER
Don't chide me!
Rather charge Mime,
for he spells danger to you.
He will lead a lad to this place,
and Fafner will fall to the boy.
I'm nothing to him,
but Mime makes him his fool.
So, fellow, mark my words!
Do whatever you like,
listen to me,
be on your guard!
The boy's not heard of the ring,
but Mime tells him the tale.

ALBERICH
You yourself will not touch the
    ring?

WANDERER
Whom I love,
I leave to his own devices.
He stands or he falls,
lord of his fate:
heroes now are my true kinsmen.

The Freedom motif reveals that
the hero beloved by Wotan is
Siegfried.

ALBERICH
Alone with Mime
I fight for the ring?

WANDERER
Only you and he
show greed for the gold.

ALBERICH
And yet I am not to succeed?

WANDERER
A hero comes
to set the hoard free.
Two Niblungs covet the gold.
Fafner falls,
he who holds the ring;
it shall pass to a new master.
Would you learn more?
Fafner lies there.

In six brief lines Wotan informs
Alberich – and us – of four main
events: the approach of a hero
who is to set the treasure free;
that Alberich's rival is his brother
Mime; that Fafner will perish; and
that the ring will be there to be
taken.

(Fafner) warnst du ihn vor dem Tod,
willig wohl liess' er den Tand.
Ich selber weck ihn dir auf.
Fafner! Fafner!
Erwache, Wurm!

ALBERICH
Was beginnt der Wilde?
Gönnt er mir's wirklich?

FAFNER
Wer stört mir den Schlaf?

WANDERER
Gekommen ist einer,
Not dir zu künden:
er lohnt dir's mit dem Leben,
Fafner lohnst du das Leben ihm
mit dem Horte, den du hütest.

FAFNER
Was will er?

ALBERICH
Wache, Fafner!
Wache, du Wurm!
Ein starker Helde naht,
Fafner dich Heilgen will er bestehn.

FAFNER
Mich hungert sein.

WANDERER
Sword Kühn ist des Kin*des* Kraft,
Ring scharf schneidet sein Schwert.

ALBERICH
Den goldnen Reif
geizt er allein:
lass mir den Ring zum Lohn,
so wend ich den Streit;
du wahrest den Hort,
Fafner und ruhig lebst du lang!

FAFNER
Ich lieg und besitz:
lasst mich schlafen!

Tell him he is to die,
and he may leave you his toys.
Observe, I shall wake him for you.
Fafner! Fafner!
Wake, dragon, wake!

ALBERICH [aside]
Is he mad enough
to bless my own business?

FAFNER
Who troubles my sleep?

WANDERER
This man here has come
to warn you of danger.
He guarantees your safety,
if you will guarantee
that he gets the golden treasure.

FAFNER
What would he?

ALBERICH
Wake up, Fafner!
Dragon, awake!
A manful hero comes,
to measure his might against
    yours.

FAFNER
My belly waits.

WANDERER
Bold is the boy and strong.
Keen-edged is his sword.

ALBERICH
The golden ring
is all he craves.
Give me that golden ring;
I'll keep you from harm.
You still have the hoard,
and long will be your life.

FAFNER
I hold what I have.
Let me slumber!

Fafner sleeps. So did the gold,
before Alberich snatched it. So
did Wotan, while Walhall was
built. So did Brünnhilde, on
Wotan's command. So did Erda,
before Wotan wakened her.
So did Hagen, when his son
Alberich appeared in his dream.
So did Gutrune, while her husband Siegfried was killed.

Fafner's words remind the attent-
ive listener of Wotan's utterance,
in a similar situation, in
Rheingold:
    'Leave me alone!
    The ring is my all!'

                                    WANDERER
        Ring   Nun, Alberich, das schlug *fehl*!
                      Doch schilt mich nicht mehr
                          Schelm!
                      Dies Eine rat ich,
        Genesis   achte noch wohl:
                      alles ist nach seiner Art:
                      an ihr wirst du nichts ändern.
                      Ich lass dir die Stätte:
                      stelle dich fest!
                      Versuch's mit Mime, dem Bruder;
  Treaty   *Freedom* der Art ja versiehst du dich besser.
                      Was anders ist,
        Sword   das lerne *nun auch*!

Authority   *Sword*   *Ride*   ALBERICH
                                      Da reitet er hin
                                      auf lichtem Ross:
           Wotan's Farewell   mich lässt er in Sorg' und *Spott*!
                                      Doch lacht nur zu,
                                      ihr leichtsinniges,
                                      lustgieriges
  Curse   Göttergelichter:
                                      euch seh ich
                                      noch alle vergehn!
                                      So lang das Gold
                                      am Lichte glänzt,
           Nibelungen Hate   hält ein Wissender Wacht!
                          Fafner   Trügen wird euch *sein Trotz*.

WANDERER
Well, Alberich, that went wrong.
Belittle me no more!

But now be warned,
and listen to me.
All things go as all things must,
and fate cannot be altered.
I leave you the field,
so take a firm stand.
Do deals with Mime, your brother,
for you two are birds of a feather.
What else there is,
you also shall learn. [he disappears
into the forest]

ALBERICH
He storms on his way
on lightning steed,
and leaves me to care and shame.
Laugh on, laugh on,
you light-minded,
luxuriating
lot of immortals!
I'll see you
all off to your graves!
For while the gold
will gleam and glow,
I watch, wise and aware.
Scorn and death to you all!
[He slips into a cleft. Morning dawns.]

The Genesis motif underlines
Wotan's stark reminder of the
irresistible power of destiny,
which rules gods and mortals
alike.

Wotan's Farewell motif fore-
shadows the Wanderer's next
journey, from Fafner's forest to
Brünnhilde's rock.

II. Akt: 2. Szene

MIME

Wir sind zur Stelle;

Sanctuary   bleib hier stehn!

SIEGFRIED

Hier soll ich das Fürchten lernen?
Fern hast du mich geleitet;
eine volle Nacht im Walde
selbander wanderten wir;
nun sollst du, Mime,
mich meiden!
Lern ich hier nicht
was ich lernen soll,
allein zieh ich dann weiter;

Loge   dich endlich werd ich da *los*!

MIME

Glaube, Liebster,
lernst du heut
und hier das Fürchten nicht;
an andrem Ort,
zu andrer Zeit
schwerlich erfährst du's je.
Siehst du dort
den dunklen Höhlenschlund?
Darin wohnt

Fafner   ein gräulich wil*der* Wurm:
unmassen grimmig
ist er und gross;
ein schrecklicher Rachen
reisst sich ihm auf;
mit Haut und Haar
auf einen Happ
verschlingt der Schlimme dich
   wohl.

Act II: Scene 2

[Day breaks. Mime and Siegfried enter.
Siegfried wears his sword. Mime spies out
the land.]

MIME
We fare no further.
Stay right here.

SIEGFRIED [sits down under a lime tree]
Here am I to learn what fear is?
Far, far away you've led me.
For a whole long night in the forest
we two have wended our way.
So, Mime,
make your departure.
Can I not learn
what I long to learn,
alone shall be my journey;
good riddance, Mime, at last.

MIME
Boy, believe me.
Learn today and now
what fear can do!
No other place,
no other time
ever will teach you fear.
Can you see
that dark abysmal den?
That is where
the dreadful dragon dwells:
horrible, grisly,
hideous and grim.
His jaws are ghastly,
gaping so wide.
Your hair and hide
– one single gulp! –
the beast will swallow you whole.

The Sanctuary motif is chromatically distorted. It portrays the
dragon's uneasy slumber, and is
followed by four *fortissimo* Fafner
motifs on the kettledrums.

SIEGFRIED

Gut ist's, den Schlund ihm zu
  schliessen;
drum biet ich mich nicht dem
  Gebiss.

MIME

Giftig giesst sich
ein Geifer ihm aus:
wen mit des Speichels
Schweiss er bespeit,
dem schwinden wohl Fleisch
  und Gebein.

SIEGFRIED

Dass des Geifers Gift mich
  nicht sehre,
weich ich zur Seite dem Wurm.

MIME

Ein Schlangenschweif
schlägt sich ihm auf:
Fafner wen er damit *um*schlingt
und fest umschliesst,
dem brechen die Glieder wie
  Glas.

SIEGFRIED

Vor des Schweifes Schwang
  mich zu wahren,
Wälsungen halt ich den Argen im Aug.
Doch heisse mich das:
Fafner hat der Wurm *ein* Herz?

MIME

Fafner Ein grimmiges, hartes Herz!

SIEGFRIED

Fafner Das sitzt ihm doch
wo es jedem schlägt,
Dragon *trag* es Mann oder Tier?

MIME

Fafner Gewiss, Knabe,
da führt's auch der Wurm;
jetzt kommt dir das Fürchten
  wohl an?

SIEGFRIED
I'd love to get at his gullet,

but shall not provoke his big teeth.

MIME
Venomous spittle
vomits his throat.
Were he to belch
the slobber at you,
it shrivels you, body and bone.

Mime's description of the dragon
is masterly. The failed blacksmith
is a brilliant storyteller.

SIEGFRIED
That the venom may not infect
   me,
I'll step aside, as I fight.

MIME
His serpent's tail
swishes about.
Let him catch you with that,
so closely coiled,
your limbs then would splinter like
   glass.

SIEGFRIED
That the serpent's tail may not
   touch me,
I'll keep my eyes on the beast.
But tell me the truth:
has the brute a heart?

Siegfried listens attentively and
prepares an intelligent battle
plan.

MIME
A treacherous, hardened heart.

SIEGFRIED
It beats, I trust,
where all hearts would beat,
be it man, be it beast?

MIME
It's there, boy,
that the serpent's heart beats.
Now say, do you feel any fear?

SIEGFRIED

Nothung   *N*othung stoss ich
dem Stolzen ins Herz!
Adventure⌐ Soll das etwa Fürchten heissen?
He, du Alter!
Ist das alles,
was deine List
mich lehren kann?
Fahr deines Wegs dann weiter;
das Fürchten lern ich hier nicht.

MIME
Wart es nur ab!
Was ich dir sage,
dünke dich tauber Schall:
ihn selber musst du
hören und sehn,
die Sinne vergehn dir dann
Sanctuary⌐   *schon*!
Wenn dein Blick verschwimmt,
der Boden dir schwankt,
im Busen bang
Fafner   dein Herz er*bebt*:
dann dankst du mir, der dich
führte,
gedenkst wie Mime dich liebt.

SIEGFRIED
Du sollst mich nicht lieben!
Sagt ich dir's nicht?
Fort aus den Augen mir;
lass mich allein:
sonst halt ich's hier länger nicht
aus,
Forge⌐ fängst du von Liebe gar an!
Das eklige Nicken
und Augenzwicken,
wann endlich soll ich's
nicht mehr sehn?
Wann werd ich den Albernen los?

MIME
Ich lass dich schon:
am Quell dort lagr' ich mich.
Steh du nur hier;
steigt dann die Sonne zur Höh',
Dragon⌐ merk auf den *Wurm*,
aus der Höhle wälzt er sich her;
hier vorbei

SIEGFRIED
Nothung pierces
his arrogant heart.
I still do not know what fear is.
Listen, babbler!
Is this really all
that your cunning
can reveal?
You ought to linger no longer,
for here I never learn fear.

MIME
Just wait and see!
You think I told you
nothing but trifling tales.
Himself you have
to hear and behold.
It's then that your blood will run
    cold.
When your eyesight fails,
the forest spins round,
your breast would burst,
your heart would stop,
but for your far-sighted
    teacher,
your loving Mime, your friend.

SIEGFRIED
Your love is not wanted!
Can you not see?
Out of my sight with you!
Leave me alone!
I simply can't stand
    any more
your loathsome prattling of love.
That odious slinking,
that winking and blinking:
when shall I see
the last of it?
When shall I be rid of the rogue?

MIME
I leave you now,
to stretch my legs by the stream.
You must stay here.
Then, when the sun's in the sky,
look for the beast!
From his cave he slithers this way,
slinking by,

'I shall not present Siegfried as a
fascist hero in earnest, but rather
as a kind of Batman or Super-
man.' (Götz Friedrich, in a *Sunday
Times* interview)

biegt er dann,
am Brunnen sich zu tränken.

SIEGFRIED
Mime, weilst du am Quell,
dahin lass ich den Wurm wohl
    gehn;
Nothung stoss ich
ihm erst in die Nieren,
wenn er dich selbst dort
mit weggesoffen!
Darum, hör meinen Rat,
raste nicht dort am Quell;
kehre dich weg,
so weit du kannst,
und komm nie mehr zu mir!

MIME
Nach freislichem Streit
dich zu erfrischen,
wirst du mir wohl nicht wehren?
Rufe mich auch,
darbst du des Rates,
oder wenn dir das Fürchten
Adventure   gefällt.

Fafner und Siegfried –
Siegfried und Fafner –
o brächten beide sich um!

SIEGFRIED
Dass der mein Vater nicht ist,
wie fühl ich mich drob so froh!
Nun erst gefällt mir
der frische Wald;
nun erst lacht mir
der lustige Tag,
da der Garstige von mir
    schied,
und ich gar nicht ihn wieder seh!

Wie sah mein Vater wohl aus?
Ha! gewiss wie ich selbst:
Forge   denn wär wo von Mime ein *Sohn*,
müsst er nicht ganz
Mime gleichen?

where you stand,
to guzzle by the water.

SIEGFRIED
You just wait by the stream,
and the dragon will smell you
    out.
Nothung shall only
run through his entrails,
when the big monster
has swallowed up Mime.
Therefore, take my advice,
do not sit down by the stream.
See yourself off,
as far as you can,
and keep away from me!

MIME
But after the fight,
dainty refreshment
Mime shall serve his darling.
Call for me also,
should you need counsel,
when you've mastered the meaning
    of fear.
[Siegfried drives Mime away]
Fafner and Siegfried –
Siegfried and Fafner:
finish each other, you fiends!
[He disappears into the forest. Siegfried
stretches himself out under the lime
tree, watching Mime's departure.]

SIEGFRIED
He is no father of mine;
that thought is a joyful thought.
never before
was the wood so fair.
Now at last
can the world wear a smile,
since the loathed one has left my
    sight,
never more to come back to me.
[he is lost in thought]
My father – what was he like?
I suppose, like myself.
If Mime had sired a son,
would he not look
like his father,

Siegfried's taunting of Mime is
more witty, more sophisticated
than before. He is maturing fast.

The dragon will be unable to
teach Siegfried fear. Brünnhilde
will (Act III).

STOP HERE!! To read about Wagner's break in his composition of
the act, and of the opera, turn to
page 152.

The oscillating motion of the
lower string instruments indicates
the Forest Murmurs: rustling,
buzzing, humming, shimmering
and almost, but not quite
windless.

(Forge) | Grade so garstig,
griesig und grau,
klein und krumm,
höckrig und hinkend,
mit hängenden Ohren,
triefigen Augen – –
fort mit dem Alp!

Wälsung Ordeal | Ich mag ihn nicht mehr sehn.

Aber – wie sah
meine Mutter wohl aus?
Das – kann ich
nun gar nicht mir denken!
Der Rehhindin gleich
glänzten gewiss
ihr hell schimmernde Augen, –
nur noch viel schöner! – – –
Da bang sie mich geboren,
warum aber starb sie da?
Sterben die Menschenmütter
an ihren Söhnen
alle dahin?

Longing | Traurig wäre das, traun! – –
Ach! möcht ich Sohn

Liebesnot | meine Mutter *sehen!* – –

Liebesnot | Meine Mutter!

Freia | ein Menschenweib! –

Woodbird

Du holdes Vöglein!
Dich hört ich noch nie:
bist du im Wald hier daheim?
Verstünd ich dein süsses
    Stammeln!
Gewiss sagt es mir was, –

Woodbird | vielleicht – von der lieben Mutter?
Ein zankender Zwerg
hat mir erzählt,
der Vöglein Stammeln
gut zu verstehn,
dazu könnte man kommen:
wie das wohl möglich wär?

Hei! ich versuch's,
sing ihm nach:
auf dem Rohr tön ich ihm ähnlich!

just as repulsive,
grisly and grey,
stooping, small,
hunchbacked and hobbling,
with ears that will dangle,
eyes that will drivel –
off with the imp!
I've seen the last of him.
[He leans back and looks up at the
branches. Forest Murmurs.]
Could I but know
what my mother was like.
Alas, that
is hard to imagine.
A roe-deer, maybe,
lucid and light,
has such eyes, when they sparkle;
only far fairer.
In bitter fear she bore me;
but why did she have to die?
Must then all mothers perish,
so that their sons
may have their own lives?
That would be sad indeed.
Ah, could I look
on my mother's likeness!
My own mother –
a mortal wife.
[He sighs. Increasing Forest Murmurs.
He listens with growing interest to the
song of a bird in the branches above
him.]
You pretty warbler,
your song is so strange!
Is this green forest your home?
Who could understand your
    twitter?
It says something to me –
perhaps of my dearest mother?
An ill-natured gnome
told me a tale
of birds and bird song;
that one could learn
what they say in their singing.
How can that tale be true?
[he notices a clump of reeds near the
lime tree]
I'll be that bird's
mockingbird;
let this reed rival your piping.

'Nature lovingly reminds us that
we are part of her, like trees. And
when I feel myself as one with
Nature, I long for you.' (Wagner to
his mother, 19 September 1846)

Entrat ich der Worte,
achte der Weise,
sing ich so seine Sprache,
Sword   versteh ich wohl auch was *es*
    spricht.

Woodbird

Es schweigt und lauscht: –
Woodbird   so schwatz ich denn los!

Das tönt nicht recht;
auf dem Rohre taugt
die wonnige Weise mir nicht.
Vöglein, mich dünkt,
ich bleibe dumm:
Woodbird   von dir lernt sich's nicht leicht!

Nun schäm ich mich gar
vor dem schelmischen Lauscher:
er lugt, und kann nichts
    erlauschen.
Heida! so höre
nun auf mein Horn;
auf dem dummen Rohre
gerät mir nichts. –
Einer Waldweise,
wie ich sie nur kann,
der lustigen sollst du nun
    lauschen.
Nach lieben Gesellen
lockt ich mit ihr:
nichts Bessres kam noch
als Wolf und Bär.
Nun lass mich sehn,
wen jetzt sie mir lockt:
Horn Call   ob das mir ein lieber Gesell.

Siegfried   *Horn Call*   *Dragon*
Sword   *Horn Call*   *Dragon*

Haha! Da hätte mein Lied
mir was Liebes erblasen!
Fafner⌉ Du wärst mir ein saubrer Gesell!

FAFNER
Was ist da?

Your language I lack,
but your chanting enchants me.
If I sing as you warble,
perhaps I shall talk in your tongue.
[he cuts a reed with his sword and fashions a
pipe from it]
It stops and waits.
I'll stammer along.
[He blows on the reed, then cuts it
shorter and tries again. He shakes his head,
makes another attempt, then gives up.]
That was ill done,
and the reed is wrong
for songs such as I want to sing.
Songster, I think
I am too slow.
I shan't learn it from you.
[he listens again to the bird]
You taught me my place,
as you perch there and listen.
You watch, and I remain wordless.

Heida! Then hear
the voice of my horn.
On the feeble reed
all my labour's lost.
Let this horn's music,
my very own,
now gladden your heart with its
 glory.
For loving companions
often I called,
but all it brought me
was wolf or bear.
Now shall I see
who comes when I call.
Perhaps I shall find me a friend?
[He blows on his horn. At each sustained
note he looks expectantly at the bird.
Fafner, in the shape of a dragon, breaks
from his lair. He utters a loud yawn.
Siegfried looks at him in amazement.]
Haha! It seems that my horn
has got hold of a beauty.
A playmate, a playmate for me!

FAFNER
What is that?

Robert Donington, in his other-
wise brilliant *Wagner's Ring and
its Symbols*, suggests that
Siegfried's cutting shorter of his
reed-pipe amounts to an act of
self-castration. Arthur Jacobs
retorted, 'He could hardly cut it
longer.'

Beethoven about his Pastoral
Symphony: 'Those yellowham-
mers, nightingales and cuckoos
up there are my assistant com-
posers.'

'On my daily walks I learnt quite
new songs from birds whom I
could not see and whose names I
did not know. Their warblings I
took home with me and worked
them into the forest scene in
Siegfried.' (Wagner in *Mein
Leben*)

Wagner's stage direction: 'The
body of the dragon is a hollow
piece of framework; when it has
reached the high ground, a trap is
opened underneath it from which
a singer sings through a speaking
tube which passes up to the jaw
of the monster.'

Wild beasts seem susceptible to
the charms of music. Siegfried
plays his horn, Orpheus his lute,
and Tamino his flute, and they all
entice creatures from their lairs.

SIEGFRIED
Ei, bist du ein Tier,
das zum Sprechen taugt,
wohl liess sich von dir was lernen?
Hier kennt einer
das Fürchten nicht:
kann er's von dir erfahren?

FAFNER

Fafner Hast *du* Übermut?

SIEGFRIED
Mut oder Übermut –
was weiss ich!
Doch dir fahr ich zu Leibe,
Fafner ⌐ lehrst du das Fürchten mich nicht!

FAFNER
Trinken wollt ich:
nun treff ich auch Frass!

SIEGFRIED
Eine zierliche Fresse
zeigst du mir da:
lachende Zähne
im Leckermaul!
Gut wär es, den Schlund dir zu
    schliessen;
Fafner ⌐ dein Rachen reckt sich *zu* weit!

FAFNER
Zu tauben Reden
taugt er schlecht:
dich zu verschlingen
frommt mir der Schlund.

SIEGFRIED
Hoho! du grausam
grimmiger Kerl,
von dir verdaut sein
dünkt mich übel:
rätlich und fromm doch scheint's,
du verrecktest hier ohne Frist.

FAFNER
Fafner ⌐ Pruh! komm,
prahlendes Kind!

SIEGFRIED
If you are a beast
that will talk to me,
talk further and be my teacher.
Here is someone
who knows no fear.
How would you like to teach me?

FAFNER
Why this disrespect?

SIEGFRIED
Respect or disrespect –
what matter?
But you shall be my booty,
will you not teach me to fear.

FAFNER
Drink I came for,
but fodder I find. [he shows his teeth]

SIEGFRIED
What a dainty muzzle
must I behold:
tittering teeth
that swig their swill.
I really should shut up that
    cavern;
your jaws are open too wide.

FAFNER
For senseless talk
they serve me not.
But they can crunch you,
flesh and bone.

SIEGFRIED
Hoho! you brutish,
mischievous beast.
To fill your stomach?
I don't think so!
You would be well advised
to give up the ghost here and now.

FAFNER
Pruh! Come,
boisterous child!

The first dragon at Bayreuth was a disaster. A Camden Town manufacturer of pantomime beasts had produced the creature and shipped it across the channel in three huge sections, in three boats. Only two sections made it to Bayreuth, the head and the tail. The vital middle part was found in 1911. It had been shipped to Beirut.

In the *Volsunga Saga*, another source, Sigurd digs a pit in the monster's path. Lodged inside, he pierces the beast's heart as it lumbers across the pit.

In one of Wagner's sources, *Das Lied vom hürnen Seyfrid*, the hero tears out several trees by their roots, throws them at the dragon and sets them – and it – alight.

SIEGFRIED

Sword   *Dragon*
Dragon   *Horn Call*
Fafner   *Sword*
Siegfried   *Fafner*

Hab Acht, Brüller,
der Prah*ler naht!*

Fafner

Da lieg, neidischer Kerl!

Nibelungen Hate   Nothung trägst du im Herzen.

Horn Call   *Fafner*

FAFNER

Nibelungen Hate   *Fafner*   Wer *bist* du, kühner Knabe,
der das Herz mir traf?
Wer reizte des Kindes Mut

Curse   zu der mordlichen Tat?
Dein Hirn brütete nicht,

Siegfried   was du *voll*bracht.

SIEGFRIED

Siegfried   Viel weiss ich noch nicht,
noch nicht auch wer ich bin:
mit dir mordlich zu ringen
reiztest du selbst meinen Mut.

Fafner   *Nibelungen Hate*   **FAFNER**
Du helläugiger Knabe,
unkund deiner selbst:
wen du gemordet

Giants   meld ich *dir.*
Der Riesen ragend Geschlecht,
Fasolt und Fafner,
die Brüder fielen nun beide.

Ring   Um verfluchtes *Gold,*
von Göttern vergabt,

Dragon   traf ich Fasolt zu tot:
der nun als Wurm
den Hort bewachte,
Fafner, den letzten Riesen,

Sword   *Nibelungen Hate*   *fällte* ein rosiger *Held.*
Blicke nun hell,

Fafner   blühender Kna*be:*
der dich Blinden reizte zur Tat,

Curse   berät nun des Blühenden Tod.
Merk wie's endet: –
acht auf mich!

SIEGFRIED

Take care, growler!
The child is near!

[He draws his sword and faces Fafner
defiantly. Fafner sprays him with venom
which Siegfried avoids. Fafner swishes
his tail, but Siegfried stabs it. Fafner
rears, exposes his breast and is mortally
wounded by Siegfried's sword. Siegfried
lets go of the sword.]

Lie there, murderous brute!
Nothung sticks in your gizzard

A triple motif accompanies
Fafner's downfall: Nibelungen
Hate, Siegfried and Fafner.

FAFNER

Who is the youthful hero
who has pierced my heart?
Who wakened your boyish will
to the murderous deed?
Your brain did not devise
what you have done.

SIEGFRIED

Not much do I know,
not even who I am.
But you urged me to kill you:
you are the cause of your death.

In *Der junge Siegfried* the dying
Fafner tells Siegfried, 'You have
killed a whole world.'

FAFNER

You fair boy with the bright eyes,
stranger to yourself;
whom you have slaughtered,
hear from me.
The giants' lofty race,
Fasolt and Fafner,
the brothers, butchered are both
    now.
For that cursed gold,
bestowed by the gods,
I put Fasolt to death.
In dragon guise
upon his hoard,
Fafner, the last of the giants,
falls to a valiant boy.
Watch yourself well,
fearless young hero!
He whose words desired the deed,
even now desires your death.
Mark the ending!
Mark my words!

Wagner directs: 'The machine representing the dragon has been
pushed forwards during the com-
bat; another trap is now opened
under it, from whence the singer
of Fafner sings through a less
powerful speaking trumpet.'

SIEGFRIED

Woher ich stamme,
rate mir noch;
weise ja scheinst du,
Siegfried | Wilder, im Sterben;
rat es nach meinem Namen:
Siegfried bin ich genannt.

FAFNER

Fafner | Siegfried ... !

SIEGFRIED

Zur Kunde taugt kein Toter.–
So leite mich denn
Sword | mein leben*des* Schwert!

Woodbird | Wie Feuer brennt das Blut!

Ist mir doch fast,
als sprächen die Vöglein zu
    mir.
Nützte mir das
des Blutes Genuss?
Das seltne Vöglein hier –
horch! was singt es mir?

WALDVOGEL

Hei! Siegfried gehört
nun der Niblungen Hort!
O fänd in der Höhle
den Hort er jetzt!
Wollt er den Tarnhelm gewinnen,
der taugt ihm zu wonniger
    Tat:
doch möcht er den Ring sich
    erraten,
der macht ihn zum Walter der Welt!

SIEGFRIED

Dank, liebes Vöglein,
für deinen Rat:
gern folg ich dem Ruf.

SIEGFRIED
Who was my father?
Do not yet die!
Yours is the wisdom,
wild one, in dying.
Hear who I am, then tell me.
Siegfried, that is my name.

FAFNER
Siegfried ...!
[he sighs, rears up and expires]

SIEGFRIED
The dead can tell no tidings.
From now I'll be led
by my living sword.
[he pulls his sword from Fafner's breast,
and in doing so smears his fingers
with blood]
Like fire burns this blood!
[he listens more intently to the song of
the Woodbird, while sucking the blood
from his fingers]
Really, I think
the birds are speaking to me.

Is it because
I tasted the blood?
That wondrous bird again!
Hark, it warbles on.

WOODBIRD
Hei! Siegfried inherits
the Nibelung hoard.
O, let him discover it
in the cave!
His is the Tarnhelm whose magic
shall bring him great love and
 renown.
The ring then awaits its new
 master,
and he shall be lord of the world.

SIEGFRIED
Thanks, dearest warbler,
you counsel me well.
I'll follow your call.
[he descends into the cave, where he
disappears]

As Siegfried withdraws the blade,
the dragons blood bespatters
him. He now can understand the
bird's warning: 'Beware of Mime!'

In *Der junge Siegfried*, when
listening to the Woodbird,
Siegfried exclaims, 'It is as though
my mother sings to me!'

According to the Woodbird, the
Tarnhelm will bring Siegfried
'great love and renown'. How
ironical – it will also bring him
shame, disrepute and death.

Siegfried has slain Fafner, and is
about to kill Mime. Originally
Wagner planned to make him a
triple killer, for Siegfried was to
have seen off his father's murderer, before despatching the
dragon. The plan was dropped.

'Child Roland to the dark tower
came.' As far back as man can
remember, he has found it necessary to go out and fight the
dragon of greed, of hunger, of
disease, of lovelessness.

II. Akt: 3. Szene

ALBERICH
Wohin schleichst du
eilig und schlau,
schlimmer Gesell?

MIME
Verfluchter Bruder,
dich braucht' ich hier!
Was bringt dich her?

ALBERICH
Geizt es dich Schelm
nach meinem Gold?
Verlangst du mein Gut?

MIME
Fort von der Stelle!
Die Stätte ist mein:
was stöberst du hier?

ALBERICH
Stör ich dich wohl
im stillen Geschäft,
wenn du hier stiehlst?

MIME
Was ich erschwang
mit schwerer Müh,
soll mir nicht schwinden.

ALBERICH
Hast du dem Rhein
das Gold zum Ringe geraubt?
Erzeugtest du gar
Tarnhelm den zähen Zauber im Reif?

MIME
Wer schuf den Tarnhelm,
der die Gestalten tauscht?

Act II: Scene 3

ALBERICH
Slinking this way,
nimble and sly?
Slippery knave!

MIME
Accursed brother,
unbidden lot!
What brings you here?

ALBERICH
Is it your greed
for all my gold
and all my goods?

MIME
Off with you, ruffian!
This region is mine!
No rummaging here!

ALBERICH
Have I found out
your secret intent,
pilfering sneak?

MIME
I sowed the seeds,
with sweat and toil:
mine is the harvest.

ALBERICH
Go to the Rhine
and ask who ravished the gold.
Then look at the ring
and see my magic at work!

MIME
Who shaped the Tarnhelm,
changing the shapes of men?

In his prose draft to *Der junge Siegfried* Wagner intended to bring on a whole battalion of Nibelungs, who were to witness the quarrel between Alberich and Mime. This would have entailed a choral scene, and the plan was dropped.

Alberich and Mime are frantic beyond reason and control. The composer intensifies their hysterics by making them sing in 3-time while the orchestra plays in 4-time.

(Tarnhelm) Der sein bedurfte,
erdachtest du ihn wohl?

ALBERICH
Was hättest du Stümper
je wohl zu stampfen verstanden?
Der Zauberring
zwang mir den Zwerg erst zur
   Kunst.

MIME
Wo hast du den Ring?
Dir Zagem entrissen ihn
   Riesen!
Was du verlorst,
meine List erlangt' es für mich.

ALBERICH
Mit des Knaben Tat
will der Knicker nun knausern?
Dir gehört sie gar nicht,
der Helle ist selbst ihr Herr!

MIME
Ich zog ihn auf;
Forge für die Zucht zahlt er mir *nun*:
für Müh und Last
erlauert ich lang meinen Lohn!

ALBERICH
Für des Knaben Zucht
will der knickrige
schäbige Knecht
keck und kühn
wohl gar König nun sein?
Dem räudigsten Hund
wäre der Ring
geratner als dir:
nimmer erringst
du Rüpel den Herrscherreif!

MIME
Behalt ihn denn:
und hüt ihn wohl,
den hellen Reif!
Sei du Herr:
doch mich heisse auch Bruder!
Um meines Tarnhelms

You craved its power,
but who created it?

ALBERICH
You blundering bungler,
what did you ever accomplish?
My magic ring
forced you to master the craft.

MIME
And where is that ring?
The giants have caught it, you
    coward.
Yours is the loss,
mine the gain, by gamble and
    guile.

ALBERICH
What the boy has won,
would the knave here deny him?
It's not yours, you rascal.
The hero is now its lord.

MIME
I brought him up,
and my pains let him repay.
What cost, what care!
I've waited too long for my wage.

ALBERICH
And for rearing him,
does the beggarly,
niggardly knave
swank and swagger
and crown himself king?
The scurviest cur
has better claim
than you to the ring.
You'll never touch it,
that magical golden prize!

MIME
Well, keep it then,
but keep it safe,
that shining ring.
You be lord,
but look! I am your brother.
Give me the Tarnhelm,

Mime has hatched two scenarios
for gaining the treasure and for
Siegfried's death – the latter is
imperative, if he wishes to hang
on to his own life: Siegfried falls
to the dragon; alternatively,
Siegfried survives the dragon but
falls to Mime. The second plan
now comes into operation.

lustigen Tand
tausch ich ihn dir:
uns beiden taugt's,
teilen die Beute wir so.

ALBERICH
Teilen mit dir?
Und den Tarnhelm gar?
Wie schlau du bist!
Sicher schlief' ich
niemals vor deinen Schlingen!

MIME
Selbst nicht tauschen?
Auch nicht teilen?
Leer soll ich gehn?
Ganz ohne Lohn?
Gar nichts willst du mir lassen?

ALBERICH
Grief | *Nichts* von allem,
nicht einen Nagel
sollst du dir nehmen!

MIME
Forge | *We*der Ring noch Tarnhelm
soll dir denn taugen!
Nicht teil ich nun mehr.
Gegen dich doch ruf ich
Siegfried zu Rat
und des Recken Schwert:
der rasche Held,
der richte, Brüderchen, dich!

ALBERICH
Kehre dich um:
Ring | aus der Höhle kommt er da*her*.

MIME
Kindischen Tand
erkor er gewiss.

ALBERICH
Den Tarnhelm hält er!

MIME
Doch auch den Ring!

a trifle, a toy:
you take the rest.
Then you and I,
each of us takes his own share.

ALBERICH
Sharing with you?
And the Tarnhelm too?
How sly you are.
Never would I
sleep and be safe, you swindler.

MIME
Why not bargain?
Why not barter?
Nothing at all?
Bled to the bone?
Nothing for your own brother?

ALBERICH
Nothing! Nothing!
No, not a nail-head
shall you be given.

MIME
Neither ring nor Tarnhelm
shall then avail you.
My offer is off.
But to crush you, I'll call
Siegfried to me,
with his mighty sword.
That valiant boy
shall judge you, brother of mine.

ALBERICH
Turn round and see.
He is coming straight from the den.

MIME
Trivial toys
he will have picked up.

ALBERICH
He's got the Tarnhelm!

MIME
He's got the ring!

(Ring)
ALBERICH

Verflucht! – den Ring! –

MIME

Lass ihn den Ring dir doch geben!
Ich will ihn mir schon gewinnen.

ALBERICH

Ring

Und doch seinem Herrn
Joy soll er allein noch ge*hö*ren!

SIEGFRIED

Joy Was ihr mir nützt,
weiss ich nicht:
Rhinegold doch *nahm* ich euch
aus des Horts gehäuftem Gold,
weil guter Rat mir es riet.
So taug eure Zier
als des Tages Zeuge:
mich mahne der Tand,
Sword *dass* ich kämpfend Fafner erlegt,
Ring doch das *Fürch*ten noch nicht
gelernt!

WALDVOGEL

Woodbird *Hei*! Siegfried gehört
nun der Helm und der Ring!
O traute er Mime
dem Treulosen nicht!
Hörte Siegfried nur scharf
auf des Schelmen Heuchlergered':
wie sein Herz es meint,
kann er Mime verstehn;
Wälsung Ordeal *Woodbird* so nützt ihm des Blutes Ge*nuss*.

ALBERICH
Accurst! The ring?

MIME
Ask him to give you the ring then.
I know quite well how to get it.
[he slips back into the forest]

ALBERICH
The ring is my right.
I am its lord and its master.
[He disappears into the rocks. Siegfried
emerges thoughtfully from the cave with the
Tarnhelm and the ring.]

The Joy motif inaugurates a
sequence of a dozen bars first
heard in *Rheingold*. They mark
the Rhinemaidens' earlier joy in
the innocent gold, and their hope
for a return of the ring to the ele-
ments that cherished it.

SIEGFRIED
What shall I do
with these things?
When I took the stuff
from the hoard of heaped-up gold,
I followed friendly advice.
The trinkets shall serve
as my battle trophies,
to witness that I
have today put Fafner to death;
but what fear is, have I not
   learnt.
[He thrusts the Tarnhelm in his belt and puts
the ring on his finger. Growing Forest Murmurs. Siegfried listens to the Woodbird with
bated breath.]

In the Edda, one of Wagner's
sources, Siegfried understands
the language not of songbirds
but, ominously, of female eagles.

WOODBIRD
Hei! Siegfried has taken
both Tarnhelm and ring.
O, guard against Mime,
beware of his wiles.
Listen with care to the lies
of the traitor's treacherous tongue.
Mime's secret mind
you will readily read.
Be blest, you have tasted the blood!
[Siegfried's demeanour shows that he has
grasped the meaning of the song. Seeing
Mime approaching, he remains motionless,
leaning on his sword.]

The Woodbird's warning ends
with the Wälsung Ordeal motif.
Hence Wagner's explanation for
King Ludwig: 'We hear, softly, softly, mother Sieglinde's loving concern for her son.'

MIME

Wälsung Ordeal

Er sinnt und erwägt
der Beute Wert:
weilte wohl hier
ein weiser Wandrer,
schweifte umher,
beschwatzte das Kind
mit listger Runen Rat?
Zwiefach schlau
sei nun der Zwerg:
die listigste Schlinge
leg ich jetzt aus,
dass ich mit traulichem
Trug-Gerede

Brooding betöre das trotzige Kind!

Woodbird *Treaty* Willkom*men, Sieg*fried!

Sag, du Kühner,
hast du das Fürchten gelernt?

SIEGFRIED

Brooding Den Lehrer fand ich noch nicht.

MIME

Doch den Schlangenwurm,

Woodbird du hast *ihn* erschlagen?

Das war doch ein schlimmer
    Gesell?

SIEGFRIED

So grimm und tückisch er war,
sein Tod grämt mich doch schier,
da viel üblere Schächer
unerschlagen noch leben.
Der mich ihn morden hiess,
den hass ich mehr als den Wurm.

MIME

Nur sachte! nicht lange
siehst du mich mehr:
zum ewgen Schlaf
schliess ich die Augen dir bald!
Wozu ich dich brauchte,
hast du vollbracht;
jetzt will ich nur noch
die Beute dir abgewinnen:–
mich dünkt, das soll mir gelingen;

Wälsung Ordeal zu betören bist du ja *leicht*!

MIME

He wonders, and weighs
the booty's worth.
Can he have met
some wise old wanderer,
roaming this way,
beguiling the boy
with tales from ancient lore?
Doubly sly
must I be now.
A treacherous ambush
have I prepared.
Friendliest falsehood
and smooth-tongued talk
shall catch out the obstinate boy.
Be welcome, Siegfried!
Say, bold fellow,
have you been taught how to fear?

SIEGFRIED

Such teacher does not exist.

MIME

But the dragon fiend –
I hope you have killed him.
A mighty old monster was he?

SIEGFRIED

Though he was grisly and grim,
I grieve over his death,
while more rascally wretches
still keep going unslaughtered.
Him who provoked the deed
I hate far more than the beast.

MIME

Have patience! You will not
see me again.
In endless sleep
shall your eyes be sealed by me.
I set you a task,
and done is the deed.
Now all that remains
for me, is to filch the treasure.
And that, I think, will be easy,
for you always have been a fool.

The Wälsung Ordeal motif again.
Siegfried has two guardian
angels, the Woodbird and his
mother Sieglinde.

SIEGFRIED

Woodbird | So sinnst du auf meinen *Schaden?*

MIME
Wie sagt ich denn das?
Siegfried, hör doch, mein
    Söhnchen!
Dich und deine Art
hasst ich immer von Herzen;
aus Liebe erzog ich
dich Lästigen nicht:
dem Horte in Fafners Hut,
dem Golde galt meine Müh.
Gibst du mir das
gutwillig nun nicht:
Siegfried, mein Sohn,
das siehst du wohl selbst –

Brooding   *Forge* | dein Leben musst du mir *las*sen!

SIEGFRIED
Dass du mich hassest,

Woodbird | *hör ich* gern:
doch auch mein Leben muss ich
    dir lassen?

MIME
Das sagt ich doch nicht?

Forge   *Crocodile* | Du verstehst mich ja *falsch!*

Crocodile | Sieh, du bist müde
von harter Müh;
brünstig wohl brennt dir der Leib:
dich zu erquicken
mit queckem Trank,
säumt ich Sorgender nicht.
Als dein Schwert du dir branntest,
braut' ich den Sud:
trinkst du nun den,
gewinn ich dein trautes Schwert
und mit ihm Helm und Hort.

Woodbird | Hihihihihi*hi*!

SIEGFRIED
So willst du mein Schwert
und was ich erschwungen,
Ring und Beute mir rauben?

SIEGFRIED
You mean then to do me mischief?

MIME
Who said that I would?
Siegfried, hear me, my loved one!

You and all your kind
have I ever truly hated.
Not love made me foster
the bothersome boy.
The treasure in Fafner's guard,
the gold is what I must have.
Either give it
willingly, or else –
Siegfried, my son,
there's no other way,
you leave me no choice – I must
   kill you!

SIEGFRIED
That I am hated,
gives me joy.
But must I also leave you my
   life-blood?

MIME
Who said that you must?
You mistake every word!
[he produces his flask and takes great pains
to hide his thoughts]
See, you are tired
with arduous toil,
flaring with fever and thirst.
Look, I have brought you
a beautiful brew,
for I know what you need.
While you hammered your sword,
I boiled you this broth.
Drink but one drop,
and mine is your glorious sword,
and Tarnhelm, gold and all!
Hihihihihihi!

SIEGFRIED
My sword you would snatch,
and all I have fought for,
ring and Tarnhelm and treasure?

Wagner informed an enquirer:
'The dragon-blood enables
Siegfried to read Mime's hidden
thoughts. Mime ... blurts out the
truth in words which contrast
with the honeyed music – a
device which is very comical.'

MIME

Was du doch falsch mich verstehst!

Brooding Stamml' ich, fasl' ich *wohl* gar?

Die grösste Mühe
geb ich mir doch,
mein heimliches Sinnen
heuchelnd zu bergen,
und du dummer Bube
deutest alles doch falsch!
Öffne die Ohren
und vernimm genau:
höre, was Mime meint!–
Hier nimm und trinke die Labung!

Mein Trank labte dich oft:
tatst du wohl unwirsch,
stelltest dich arg:
was ich dir bot –
erbost auch – nahmst du's doch
   immer.

SIEGFRIED

Einen guten Trank
hätt ich gern:
wie hast du diesen gebraut?

MIME

Hei! so trink nur:
trau meiner Kunst!
In Nacht und Nebel
sinken die Sinne dir bald;
ohne Wach und Wissen

Shuffle stracks streckst du die *Glie*der.

Liegst du nun da,
leicht könnt ich
die Beute nehmen und bergen:
doch erwachtest du je,
nirgends wär ich
sicher vor dir,

Shuffle hätt ich selbst auch den *Ring*.

Drum mit dem Schwert,
das so scharf du schufst,
hau ich dem Kind
den Kopf erst ab:
dann hab ich mir Ruh und auch
   den Ring!
Hihihihihi! Hihihihihihi!

MIME

How you do misunderstand!
Do I drivel or drool?
I keep my counsel,
taking great care
to hide in my heart
my secret meaning,
and you, silly boy,
will misinterpret my words.
Open your ears, child,
and attend to me:
this is what Mime means.
Here, boy, drink this to refresh
   you;
my draughts pleased you before.
When you are awkward,
when you are cross,
I bring you a drink.
You fuss, but never refuse it.

SIEGFRIED

A refreshing drink
would be good.
How did you brew the broth?

MIME

Hei! Just drink,
have faith in my flair.
In deathly darkness
shall all your senses be plunged.
Without mind or motion,
stretched stiff is your body.
Once you are down,
I'll easily
take the treasure and hide it.
But if you were to wake,
I would never
find myself safe,
though I pilfered the ring.
So with this sword,
with your glorious sword,
child, will I chop
your head right off.
Then shall I have rest and ring as
   well.
Hihihihihi! Hihihihihihi!

'This scene is no family entertainment. The destiny of the whole world depends on this unique, fearless hero.' (Wagner to King Ludwig, 23 February 1869)

Violins and double basses play *col legno* (with the wooden part of the bow on the string). This gives Mime's insane laughter a diabolical dimension.

SIEGFRIED
Im Schlafe willst du mich morden?

MIME
Was möcht ich? Sagt ich denn
  das? –
Ich will dem Kind
nur den Kopf abhaun!
Denn hasste ich dich
auch nicht so sehr,
und hätt ich des Schimpfs
und der schändlichen Mühe
auch nicht so viel zu rächen:
aus dem Wege dich zu räumen
darf ich doch nicht rasten,
wie käm ich sonst anders zur Beute,

Woodbird   da Alberich auch nach ihr lugt? – –
Brooding   Nun, mein *Wäl*sung!
   Wolfssohn du!
Forge   Sauf und würg dich zu Tod:
Sword   nie tust du mehr *'nen Schluck*!

SIEGFRIED
Schmeck du mein Schwert,
ekliger Schwätzer!

ALBERICH
Forge   *Brooding*   *Ha*haha Hahaha Hahaha *Ha*haha
   ha!

SIEGFRIED
Neides-Zoll
zahlt Nothung:
Curse   *Horn Call*   dazu durft ich ihn schmieden.

Grief   In der *Höh*le hier
Curse   lieg auf dem Hort!
Mit zäher List
erzieltest du ihn:
jetzt magst du des wonnigen
  walten!
Einen guten Wächter
geb ich dir auch,
Fafner   dass er vor Dieben dich *deckt*.

SIEGFRIED
I shall be slain in my slumber?

MIME
I'd slay you? I never said that!

You only shall
have your head hacked off!
So hot is my hate,
so great my grudge,
so bitter your taunts,
and so shameful my toil,
that it cries aloud for vengeance.
So, to take your life, I really
dare delay no longer.
How else could I come by the
　treasure,
since Alberich covets it too?
Now, my Wälsung,
wolf-begot,
drink and choke to death!
You'll never drink again.
[Seized by violent revulsion, Siegfried aims a
swift blow at Mime, who falls dead. From the
rocks Alberich's mocking laughter is heard.]

The Wanderer's prediction has
come true: Mime has lost his
head to him who does not know
fear.

SIEGFRIED
Savour my sword,
prating impostor!

ALBERICH
Hahaha hahaha, hahaha hahaha
　ha!

Two murders inaugurate
Siegfried's maturity.

SIEGFRIED
Greed's reward
pays Nothung.
That is why I had forged it.
[he carries Mime's body to the cave]
In the dragon's lair
lie on the hoard.
Your stubborn guile
has gained you the gold,
and now you are lord of its lustre.

And a weighty watchman
you shall have too,
keeping marauders at bay.

Dragon		Da lieg auch du,
	Ring	dunkler Wurm!
		Den gleissenden Hort
		hüte zugleich
		mit dem beuterührigen Feind:

Forge   *Fafner*   so fandet ihr beide nun Ruh!

Horn Call
Heiss ward mir
von der harten Last! –
Brausend jagt
mein brünstges Blut.
Die Hand brennt mir am Haupt. –
Hoch steht schon die Sonne:
aus lichtem Blau
blickt ihr Aug
auf den Scheitel steil mir herab. –
Linde Kühlung
Woodbird erkies ich under der *Linde*!

Longing
Noch einmal, liebes Vöglein,
da wir so lang
lästig gestört, –
lauscht' ich gerne deinem Sange:
auf dem Zweige seh ich
wohlig dich wiegen;
zwitschernd umschwirren
dich Brüder und Schwestern,
umschweben dich lustig und lieb!
Doch ich – bin so allein,
hab nicht Bruder noch Schwester.
Meine Mutter schwand,
mein Vater fiel:
Forge nie sah sie der Sohn! –
Mein einzger Gesell
war ein garstiger Zwerg;
Güte zwang
uns nie zu Liebe;
listige Schlingen
warf mir der Schlaue:–
nun musst ich ihn gar erschlagen!–
Freundliches Vöglein,
Longing dich frage ich nun:
gönntest du mir
wohl ein gut Gesell?
Willst du mir das Rechte raten?

[with a great effort he pushes the
dragon's body to the entrance of the cave,
blocking it up completely]
Lie by his side,
hapless beast.
The glittering gold,
guarded by you
and by him who craved for the
    hoard.
Thus from their labour both may
    rest.
Hot am I
with my heavy toil.
Fever fires
my boiling blood.
My hand burns on my brow –
hot sunlight above me.
In azure glow
glares its eye
on my temple, steadfast and steep.
Shade and shelter
await me under the lime tree.
[he reclines under the lime tree]
Once more then, dearest warbler,
now that we won
calm and content,
let me listen to your singing.
On your branch I see you
blissfully swaying.
Chirping and carolling
brothers and sisters
surround you in dulcet delight.
But I am so alone,
have no brothers or sisters;
and my mother died,
my father fell,
unknown to their son.
My only companion
a pestilent dwarf.
Love nor kindness
did he kindle.
Treacherous traps
he set to ensnare me,
and so I was forced to slay him.
Sweetest of songsters,
I beg of you now:
go and find
a faithful friend for me.
Will you be my guide and
    guardian?

Fafner's motivic interval was originally the perfect fourth. In
dragon's guise this grew into an
augmented fourth, the *tritonus
diabolus*. After his death an addi-
tional semitone makes it a perfect
fifth. His life spans perfection,
diabolism and perfection.

The fatherless and motherless lad
is alone in the world, like the
Dutchman, like Tristan, like Parsifal, like Richard Wagner (whose
spiritual loneliness was his
creative strength).

	Ich lockte so oft,
(Longing)	und erlost es mir nie:
	du, mein Trauter,
	träfst es wohl besser!
	So recht ja rietest du schon:
	nun sing! ich lausche dem Gesang.

WALDVOGEL

Woodbird *Hei*! Siegfried erschlug
nun den schlimmen Zwerg!
Jetzt wüsst ich ihm noch
das herrlichste Weib.
Auf hohem Felsen sie schläft,

Feuer umbrennt ihren Saal:
durchschritt er die Brunst,
weckt' er die Braut,
Brünnhilde wäre dann sein!

SIEGFRIED

O holder Sang!
Süssester Hauch!
Wie brennt sein Sinn
mir sehrend die Brust!
Wie zückt er heftig
zündend mein Herz!
Was jagt mir so jach
durch Herz und Sinne?
Sing es mir, süsser Freund!

WALDVOGEL

Woodbird *Lus*tig im Leid
sing ich von Liebe;
wonnig aus Weh
web ich mein Lied:
nur Sehnende kennen den Sinn!

SIEGFRIED

Fort jagt mich's
jauchzend von hinnen,
Loge fort aus dem Wald auf den *Fels*! –
Noch einmal sage mir,
holder Sänger:
werd ich das Feuer durchbrechen?
Sanctuary Kann ich erwecken die Braut?

WALDVOGEL

Woodbird *Die* Braut gewinnt,
Brünnhild erweckt

I've longed many times,
many times have I lost.
You, my faithful,
you will not fail me.
You always counselled me well.
Now sing! I listen to your song.

WOODBIRD
Hei! Siegfried has killed
the deceitful dwarf.
Now let him secure
a glorious bride!
She sleeps where rocks rise up
    high.
Fires encircle the fell.
Who masters the flames,
wakens the maid,
Brünnhilde wins he for wife.

SIEGFRIED
O words of joy!
Sweetest of songs!
Its promise burns
like fire in my breast.
My will awakes,
aflame is my heart.
What courses so swift
through heart and senses?
Speak to me, sweetest friend!

WOODBIRD
Glad is my grief,
love is my music.
Sweetness and woe
warbles my song,
and lovers alone understand.

SIEGFRIED
Forth, onward,
forth and rejoicing,
forth from the woods to the fell!
But once more speak to me,
wondrous warbler.
Sing, shall I fare through the fire?
Shall I awaken the bride?

WOODBIRD
Who wakes and wins
Brünnhild for bride,

'Brünnhilde wäre dann sein'
('Brünnhilde wins he for wife'):
these words are Siegfried's life-
and-death motto. Now they send
him on a journey of joy. When he
repeats the same words to the
brutal Hagen, in *Götterdämmerung*, they become his death
warrant.

(Woodbird) ein Feiger nie:
nur wer das Fürchten nicht kennt!

SIEGFRIED
Der dumme Knab,
der das Fürchten nicht kennt,
mein Vöglein, der bin ja ich!
Noch heut gab ich
vergebens mir Müh,
das Fürchten von Fafner zu lernen.
Nun brenn ich vor Lust,
es von Brünnhild zu wissen:
wie find ich zum Felsen den Weg?

SIEGFRIED
So wird mir der Weg gewiesen!

Wohin du flatterst,
Woodbird folg ich dem Flug!

no coward he!
Only a man without fear!

SIEGFRIED
The foolish boy,
the young lad without fear,
dear songster, why, I am he!
This very day
I have tried in vain
to find out from Fafner what fear is.
I now burn with longing
to learn it from Brünnhild.
What way shall I take to the fell?
[the bird flutters up, circles above Siegfried,
and then flies off]

SIEGFRIED
Now I see the path before me,
[joyously]
and where you guide me,
there shall I fly.
[He follows the bird which teases him for a
time, leading him in various different direc-
tions. Then it decides on a definite course
and flies towards the back. Siegfried follows.]

Siegfried's ornithological connec-
tions are remarkable. A bird
warns him of his death at Mime's
hands; it shows him the way to
Brünnhilde; it seems to him to
deputize for his mother; and birds
play an important part – in the
shape of ravens – at his death, in
another forest. Ironically, before
Hagen kills him, he states, 'I listen
to songs of women, and hushed
are the songs of birds.'

Siegfried Abandoned!

That is what Wagner did in the second scene of Act II (p. 118–9), when he interrupted his Orchestral Sketch with the scribbled note, 'When shall we see each other again?' The day was 27 June 1857.

Wagner had embarked on the *Ring* in October 1848, with his preliminary study *Die Nibelungensage* (*Mythus*); four years later the whole *Ring* poem (libretto) was completed. He needed less than two years for each of his next steps, the composition of *Rheingold* and *Walküre*. On the last day of March 1857 he completed the first full score of Act I of *Siegfried*, and on his forty-fourth birthday, 22 May 1857, he began working on the second act. One might, therefore, reasonably expect the completion of the whole tetralogy by 1860 or thereabouts. In reality, the last bars of *Götterdämmerung* were to be written as late as November 1874!

A brief chronology provides the following facts, though none of the reasons for the interruption of the *Ring*:

27 June 1857	Work on *Siegfried* abandoned
13 July 1857	Work on *Siegfried* resumed
9 August 1857	Orchestral draft of Act II completed
20 August 1857	Prose draft of *Tristan und Isolde* begun
6 August 1859	*Tristan und Isolde* completed
24 October 1867	*Die Meistersinger von Nürnberg* completed
1 March 1869	Work on *Siegfried* (Act III) resumed
5 February 1871	*Siegfried* completed
21 November 1874	*Götterdämmerung* completed

Commentators have offered a range of explanations for Wagner's unexpected disavowal of one work in favour of two others. A change of direction in mid-career was unprecedented, but was it unpremeditated? Let us examine the relevant circumstances.

1. A whole year before Wagner switched so momentously from *Siegfried* to *Tristan* – he had just finished work on *Walküre* – he jotted down this remarkable phrase (on 21 May 1856):

Sangst _____ du mir nicht _____ , dein Wis - sen sei das

Leuch - ten der Lie - - - - be zu mir?

The words are those of *Siegfried* (Act III), but the music, with its chromatic ascent, belongs unmistakably to Brangäne's plea in the first act of *Tristan*, which Wagner was to compose a year and a half later.

2. On 18 December 1856 – while working on the first act of *Siegfried* – Wagner composes eighteen bars of music in piano score, which he heads 'Liebesszene T und I'. Here is the beginning:

Pure second act *Tristan*, anticipated by seventeen months.

3. On the same day he informs the Princess Marie Wittgenstein, 'Today I intended to continue working on *Siegfried*, but all of a sudden I found myself working on *Tristan*.'

4. Only three days later, on 22 December 1856, he admits to Otto Wesendonck, 'I have lost my appetite for *Siegfried*, and my musical intuition tends to stray in a different direction altogether. My present mood belongs in the realm of melancholy, of *Schwermut*.'

5. In the second complete draft of *Siegfried*, Act II, he scribbles those words mentioned at the start of this essay, to the effect that work on the *Ring* was to be shelved.

6. Next day he discloses to Liszt, 'I have torn *Siegfried* out of my heart and have locked him up securely ... As for *Tristan*, absolute and total silence!!!'

7. So far, Wagner's clues have been unspecific, but in his letter of 4 July 1857 to Frau Julie Ritter he explains, 'I have left Siegfried alone in the forest for one year, in order to find my feet with *Tristan und Isolde*, which I intend to perform next summer in Strasbourg.'

8. At that time, in summer 1857, he enters a brief observation in his diary (*Annalen*) which almost takes one's breath away: 'Interruption of *Siegfried* in favour of *Tristan und Isolde* is decided. Message to Emperor of Brazil. (*Tristan* Italian–Brazilian).'

9. It is generally assumed that Wagner abandoned his work on the second act of *Siegfried*, then resumed his labour three weeks later in order to complete the act, before giving his undivided attention to *Tristan*. Alas, such single-mindedness was not available to Wagner at that time. The encounter with Mathilde Wesendonck had not only provided inspiration for his work, but intoxication for his senses and turmoil in his heart. Witness his *cri de coeur* to Marie Wittgenstein of August 1857: 'The second act is finished. Fafner is dead, and Siegfried has run after the Woodbird, but while working on *Siegfried*, *Tristan* has given me no peace. In fact, I have been working simultaneously on both.'

So much for the external evidence. Ostensibly Wagner put aside his *Ring* in order to devote a little time – one year at most – to the production of *Tristan und Isolde*, which he intended to perform in Strasbourg and, translated into Italian, in South America. Why South America?

King Ludwig's patronage of Wagner has become legendary, but little detail has emerged about the plans of Dom Pedro II of Brazil, who might easily have played a role in Wagner's life similar to that of the King of Bavaria. This cultured, artistic-ally-minded member of the royal house of the Bragancas of Portugal enquired of Wagner, through his Dresden consul Dr Ferreira-Franca, whether the composer would come to Rio de Janeiro and perform his works there. The offer reached Wagner in March 1857. Dr Ferreira-Franca also suggested that Wagner might consider dedicating the *Ring* to the emperor, who would then sponsor its performances (in Italian). In his reply Wagner regretted that, in order to be fully understood, the *Ring* could only be performed on the soil from which it had sprung, and only in its original language. To avoid offending his prospective protector, Wagner despatched a triple gift to Dom Pedro, a magnificently bound triptych – the piano scores of

Der fliegende Holländer, Tannhäuser and *Lohengrin*. He also offered to dedicate to the emperor an entirely new work, as yet unwritten. That work was *Tristan und Isolde*. And here the Brazilian trail peters out. We do not know what circumstances conspired to keep Pedro from *Isolde*. The fact remains that, by the summer of 1857, the *Ring* project had been abandoned in favour of the more readily composable, marketable and performable *Tristan und Isolde*.

Have we at last found the reason for Wagner's switch from the *Ring* to *Tristan*? Was the selling power of *Tristan* not the reason for abandoning the *Ring*, but its agreeable consequence? At any rate, *Tristan* must have called loudly for its creator. Mathilde Wesendonck, Wagner's beloved muse, had done her inspirational duty for the throbs and thrills of *Walküre*, but *Siegfried* had its being on a different emotional plane. Wagner's own *Weltschmerz* ('My present mood belongs in the realm of melancholy'), arising partly from the unattainability of Mathilde, agitated him away from the projected C major jubilation of *Siegfried* towards *Tristan*'s sombre chromaticism. Furthermore, his discovery of the teachings of Schopenhauer confirmed his own recently acquired philosophy of life, namely the advisability of accepting, nay willing the inevitable: a proposition as relevant to the essence of *Tristan* as it is alien to the heroics of *Siegfried*.

We have assembled a cluster of considerations which combined to entice Wagner away from the *Ring*. Yet, as always in his creative life, he seems to steer – or be steered? – towards the task for which he was ready. When at the peak of his power, and when that peak coincided with his mental attunement to the material, he produced *Tristan*; and when he had gained wisdom which comes with age, he turned to *Meistersinger*. The third act of *Siegfried* had to await its composer's sang-froid, which was to enable him to cope with the emotional turmoil engendered by Wotan's annihilation and by the ecstatic union of Siegfried and Brünnhilde. Fifteen years earlier this might have finished him. Now he was able to finish it.

To a certain extent, the switch from the *Ring* to *Tristan* was a *quid pro quo*. Numerous themes of the one were transferred to the other:

Ring	Tristan
Siegfried's father dies after his conception	Tristan's father dies after his conception
Siegfried's mother dies at his birth	Tristan's mother dies at his birth

Siegfried fights the man (Wotan), who tries to prevent him from gaining access to Brünnhilde	Tristan fights the man (Morold), who tries to prevent him from gaining access to Isolde
Love obliterates allegiance: BRÜNNHILDE Farewell, Walhall's glittering world! In dust may sink its glorious walls!	Love obliterates allegiance: TRISTAN What dream was mine of Tristan's honour? ISOLDE What dream was mine of Isolde's shame?
Brünnhilde's healing powers	Isolde's healing powers
Siegfried's boat voyage	Tristan's boat voyage
The potion causes oblivion, love and eventual death	The potion causes oblivion, love and eventual death
A king (Gunther), unable to win a bride for himself, lets his bloodbrother (Siegfried) procure the woman (Brünnhilde) who is destined for the procurer	A king (Mark), unable to win a bride for himself, lets his nephew (Tristan) procure the woman (Isolde) who is destined for the procurer
Siegfried leaves Brünnhilde and returns as suitor on behalf of another (King Gunther)	Tristan leaves Isolde and returns as suitor on behalf of another (King Mark)
Siegfried assumes a false name, Gunther	Tristan assumes a false name, Tantris
The loveless marriage of King Gunther and Brünnhilde	The loveless marriage of King Mark and Isolde
Brünnhilde's love turns to hatred	Isolde's love turns to hatred
Siegfried's dying vision of Brünnhilde	Tristan's dying vision of Isolde
Brünnhilde's *Liebestod*	Isolde's *Liebestod*

One final observation:

This theme occurred to Wagner while composing the shepherd's jubilant music of the third act of *Tristan*. He then decided to save the theme for the third act of *Siegfried*, where it eventually found its rightful place (as the Liebesbund motif); and with it we have rounded the circle and are ready to return to *Siegfried*, Act III.

Siegfried, having slain the dragon, listens to the bird's advice; illustration by Ludwig Burger (1876)

Brünnhilde awakes; illustration by
Knut Ekwall (1876)

III
Act

Synopsis
Leitmotifs
Libretto

Act III: Story

The Foot of Brünnhilde's Rock

Scene 1
The Wanderer calls up Erda to consult her about the future. When she advises him to seek guidance from Brünnhilde instead, he tells her of their daughter's disobedience and punishment. Erda is dismayed and wishes to be released from his spell, but the Wanderer wants to know how the gods' downfall may be averted. Erda is unwilling to prolong the discussion, and the Wanderer announces that he is about to bequeath the world to Siegfried. With that he allows Erda to descend.

Scene 2
Siegfried approaches. The Wanderer's questions about the sword, its origin, its splinters and its reforging, irritate Siegfried, and at last he bids the 'ancient meddler' to take himself off. Wotan bars Siegfried's way with his outstretched spear, which Siegfried shatters, imagining that the Wanderer was in fact the murderer of Siegmund, Siegfried's father. Wotan picks up the splinters of his spear and vanishes.

On Brünnhilde's Rock

Scene 3
Sounding his horn, Siegfried plunges into the wall of fire. He finds the sleeping Brünnhilde and wakens her with a kiss. She welcomes him rapturously, but soon realizes that her loss of godhood has made her a mortal woman, subject to her new master's impetuosity. Her longing for her deliverer, however, has become so irresistible that she surrenders to her destiny – 'Living in love, triumphant in death!'

Siegfried blows his horn before
plunging into the wall of fire
to rescue Brünnhilde.

Act III: Action

1. Orchestra: Prelude
2. The Wanderer wakens Erda
3. The Wanderer is defeated by Siegfried
4. Siegfried penetrates the fire
5. Siegfried wakens Brünnhilde
6. Brünnhilde greets Siegfried
7. Brünnhilde recoils from Siegfried
8. Brünnhilde and Siegfried's joyful union

Siegfried meets the Wanderer;
set design by Joseph Hoffman,
Bayreuth 1876

Act III: Leitmotifs

The leitmotifs new to the act follow in chronological order, together with the page number of first appearance.

Bequest   p.174

Revival   p.198

Hosanna   p.198

Jubilation   p.200

Idyll   p.208

Liebesglück   p.208

(teurig, doch zart.)

O   Sieg - fried, Herr - li - cher! Hort ___ der Welt!

Liebesbund   p.212

Commentary on the Leitmotifs

Bequest

This is first heard in Wotan's scene with Erda, when the god bequeathes the world to Siegfried: 'The valiant Wälsung shall now inherit my reign.' Commentators have found a whole variety of names for this motif, such as 'Inheritance', 'Heritage of the World', 'Resignation' (imprecise) and 'Siegfried's Tender Love for Brünnhilde and Hers for Him' (goodness!). Violins, oboes, clarinets and horns sound the first note of the motif, *fortissimo*; on its second note it fades to *piano*, and then a mighty crescendo ends in an impressive *fortissimo*. Wagner said of this motif that it should sound 'like the proclamation of a new religion'.

Revival

The usual name for this motif is 'Brünnhilde's Awakening'. Wagner suggests, however, more than a mere awakening: with Siegfried's kiss, Brünnhilde is reborn as a mortal woman. Four chords constitute the Revival motif. The first (E minor, *forte*) is played by oboes, clarinets and horns; the second (C major, *pianissimo*) by flutes, cor anglais, trumpets, trombones and timpani; then follow harp arpeggios and high violin trills; the third chord (E minor, *forte*) is the same as the first; the final chord (D minor, *pianissimo*) has the same instrumentation as the second and is followed, as before, by harp arpeggios and high violin trills.

Hosanna

'Hosanna' is defined by the dictionary as a 'shout of adoration'; here it is sung by Siegfried to the words, 'I bless my mother, giving me life!' The second half of the motif, from its fourth note onwards, is identical to the Liebe-Tragik motif. This motif is usually called 'Love's Greeting'. We prefer the shorter and more pertinent name. (There used to be a whole ragbag of 'Love's ...' motifs, such as 'Love's Fascination', 'Love's Rapture', 'Love's Peace', 'Love's Resolution', 'Love's Happiness', 'Love's Longing', 'Love's Joy', 'Love's Determination', 'Conjugal Love', 'Redemption Through Love' and 'Wälsungen Love'.)

Jubilation

Woodwind, horns and sweeping harp arpeggios announce this ecstatic motif. The precise dotted rhythm and the thrice repeated bar which constitute the motif turn this short phrase into a fanfare. Former designations, such as 'Love's Rapture', 'Love's Passion' and 'Enthusiasm of Love' have been discarded in favour of brevity.

Idyll

First conceived in 1864, this peaceful motif was designed for an unwritten string quartet, which was to contain motifs of a special and private significance to the composer and his adored Cosima. Five years later, in 1869, the motif was used in the final act of *Siegfried* and re-used, in December 1870, in the *Siegfried Idyll*:

In the opera, *Siegfried*, the motif is extended and ends on the falling seventh, thus foreshadowing the Brünnhilde motif in *Götterdämmerung*:

Liebesglück

The two final motifs have been given German names, partly to avoid lengthy titles, but chiefly for semantic reasons. 'Liebesglück' (the euphoric mood enduced by mutual feeling of compatibility and of security) is a term which German Romantic poets used freely and fondly. The motif is built on the A flat major chord, but its first note is a chromatic, sustained B natural. Like the Idyll motif, it was to have appeared in the string quartet, then was used in the *Siegfried Idyll* instead. In the latter it is in triple time, begins on a trill and is announced by clarinet. In the opera it is in four-four time, is announced by the voice and violins and has no initial trill. Compare the above motif with the *Idyll* version:

Liebesbund

The German Romantic term means a bond of love, freely accepted by consenting lovers. Amongst its former titles are 'Love's Resolution', 'Decision to Love', 'Love's Determination' and 'Love's Union'. It was originally designed for the third act of *Tristan* but was then used in both *Siegfried* and the *Siegfried Idyll*. In both cases, shape and key are identical, but in the opera it is announced by a single horn, in the *Idyll* by two.

Carl Doepler's costume design for
the Wanderer (Wotan), Bayreuth
1876

Ride   Erda   *Wotan's Frustration*
Treaty   *Erda*   *Götterdämmerung*
Wanderer   *Erda*   *Götterdämmerung*
Grief   *Erda*   *Ride*
Oblivion   *Fate*   *Treaty*
Fate   *Treaty*

III. Akt: 1. Szene

Vorspiel

WANDERER
Wache! Wache!
Liebesnot — *Wa*la, erwach!
Aus langem Schlaf
weck ich dich Schlummernde
  wach.
Liebesnot — Ich rufe dich auf:
Erda — herauf! her*auf*!
Aus nebliger Gruft,
aus nächtigem Grunde herauf!
Erda! Erda!
Ewiges Weib!
Genesis — Aus heimischer Tiefe
tauche zur Höh!
Dein Wecklied sing ich,
dass du erwachest;
aus sinnendem Schlafe
sing ich dich auf.
Götterdämmerung — All*wiss*ende!
Genesis — Urwelt*weis*e!
Erda! Erda!
Liebesnot — Ewiges Weib!
Wache, erwache, du Wala!
Treaty —   Er*wa*che!

Fate   *Oblivion* — **ERDA**
Stark ruft das Lied;
kräftig reizt der Zauber;
ich bin erwacht
aus wissendem Schlaf;
Fate — wer scheucht den Schlummer mir?

Act III: Scene 1

Prelude

[A wild region at the foot of a rocky mountain. Stormy night with thunder and lightning. The Wanderer appears. He strides to a cavernous opening in a rock, leans on his spear and calls into the cave.]

WANDERER
Waken, Wala!
Wala, awake!
From timeless sleep
open your slumbering eyes.

I call you to life.
Arise! Arise!
From mist-riven caves,
from fathomless canyons, arise!
Erda! Erda!
Woman divine!
From earthbound abode
now rise to the light!
My song shall wake you,
and you shall answer.
Your farsighted wisdom
will I awake.
All-knowing one,
well of wisdom,
Erda! Erda!
Woman divine!
Waken, awaken, you Wala,
   awaken! [Bluish light glows in the cave.
Erda rises slowly from below.]

ERDA
Mighty your song.
Potent magic moves me.
Who haunts my sleep,
my clear-sighted sleep?
Who dares to break my dream?

The orchestral prelude portrays Wotan as the restless, vigorous god. No longer is he merely an observer, as in Acts I and II; he reverts to his archetypal model, *Wuotan*, the raging god. Conflicting emotions (discussed in the course of this act) propel him into two critical confrontations, first with Erda, then with Siegfried. Both will have consequences of catastrophic proportions. Wagner uses a prodigality of leitmotifs in the prelude, signifying the turmoil in Wotan's mind.

Composed in 1869, this act profits from Wagner's post-*Tristan* and post-*Meistersinger* technique of supreme orchestral and vocal virtuosity.

'Speaking to you about *Siegfried* means speaking of a dark, exalted and awesome dread which accompanies me into the realm of my third act ... the core of the great world tragedy. The world is on the brink of destruction, and the god attempts to ensure a universal rebirth, for Wotan personifies the world's will to exist. Everything here is sublime terror, and I cannot do other than express it in riddles.' (Wagner to King Ludwig)

Wotan's love for the world (in *Rheingold*) which turned to horror (in *Walküre*) now becomes anxiety for its survival. *Liebe* has changed into *Not*, hence Wotan's awakening of Erda, mother of Brünnhilde, to the *Liebesnot* motif.

Agitated woodwind and strings, aided by sombre trombones, hint at Wotan's newly found impetuosity, which is to launch him into his later duel with Siegfried.

WANDERER

Erda

Der *Weck*rufer bin ich,

Götterdämmerung

und *Wei*sen üb ich,

dass *weit*hin wache

was fester Schlaf verschliesst.

Wanderer

Die *Welt* durchzog ich,

wanderte viel,

Genesis

*Kun*de zu werben,

urweisen Rat zu gewinnen.

Kundiger gibt es

keine als dich:

bekannt ist dir,

was die Tiefe birgt,

was Berg und Tal,

Luft und Wasser durchwebt.

Wo Wesen sind,

wehet dein Atem;

wo Hirne sinnen,

haftet dein Sinn;

alles, sagt man,

Liebesnot

sei dir bekannt.

Dass ich nun Kunde gewänne,

Treaty

weck ich dich aus dem *Schlaf.*

Oblivion

ERDA

Mein Schlaf ist Träumen,

mein Träumen Sinnen,

Genesis

mein Sinnen Walten des *Wis*sens.

Doch wenn ich schlafe,

wachen die Nornen:

sie weben das Seil,

und spinnen fromm was ich weiss:

was frägst du nicht die Nornen?

WANDERER

Im Zwange der Welt

Ring

weben die *Nor*nen:

Liebe-Tragik

sie können *nichts* wenden noch

wandeln;

doch deiner Weisheit

Liebesnot

dankt ich den *Rat* wohl,

wie zu hemmen ein rollendes Rad.

ERDA

Ring

*Männer*taten

umdämmern mir den Mut;

Liebe-Tragik

mich Wissende *selbst*

Walhall

bezwang ein Waltender *einst.*

Ein Wunschmädchen

WANDERER
Your dream breaker am I.
The songs I utter
are lordly rousers,
unlocking sleep-sealed eyes.
The wide world ranging,
wandering far,
searching for knowledge,
wisdom I wanted to win me.
Wiser than Erda
is none on earth.
To you is known
what the deeps conceal,
what hill and dale,
wind and water contain.
Where life is lived,
there lives your spirit.
Where brains are brooding,
there broods your thought.
Fount of foresight,
woman most wise:
that I may win me your wisdom,
have I broken your sleep.

ERDA
My sleep is dreaming,
my dreaming delving,
my delving weaving of wisdom.
But while I slumber,
Norns keep vigil,
by winding their rope
and weaving all that I know.
Go ask the Norns for knowledge.

WANDERER
In thrall to the world
Norns do their weaving,
unable to alter what must be.

To you I come now.
Counsel me how
to arrest a wheel on the roll.

ERDA
Men's endeavours
bedim and daze my mind.
The wise one herself
surrendered her will to the god.
A wish-maiden

Previously, Wotan had been content to accept – and indeed to promote – the various decrees of destiny. Now he makes one final, impetuous attempt to 'arrest a wheel on the roll'.

(Walhall)	gebar ich Wotan:
	der Helden Wal
Ride	hiess für sich er sie küren.
Sanctuary	Kühn *ist* sie
Fate	und weise auch:
	was weckst du mich,
	und frägst um Kunde
Walhall *Wotan's Child*	nicht Erdas und Wotans *Kind?*

WANDERER

Wotan's Child	Die Walküre meinst du,
	Brünnhild, die Maid?
	Sie trotzte dem Stürme-
	bezwinger;
	wo er am stärksten selbst sich
	bezwang,
	was den Lenker der Schlacht
	zu tum verlangte,
	doch dem er wehrte
	– zuwider sich selbst –;
	allzu vertraut
	wagte die Trotzige
Ride	das für sich zu vollbringen,
	Brünnhild in brennender Schlacht.
	Streitvater
Death	*straf*te die Maid;
	in ihr Auge drückte er Schlaf;
	auf dem Felsen schläft sie fest:
	erwachen wird
	die Weihliche nur,
Liebe-Tragik	um einen *Mann* zu minnen als
	Weib.
Fate *Wotan's Farewell*	*Fromm*ten mir Fragen an *sie?*

ERDA

Wotan's Farewell	Wirr wird mir,
	seit ich erwacht;
	wild und kraus
Oblivion	kreist die *Welt!*
	Die Walküre,
	der Wala Kind,
	büsst in Banden des Schlafs,
Fate *Wotan's Child*	als die *wiss*ende Mutter *schlief?*

	Der den Trotz lehrte,
	strafst den Trotz?
Fate	Der die Tat entzündet,
	zürnt um die Tat?
	Der die Rechte wahrt,

I bore to Wotan,
and manhood's prime
he bade her bring him to Walhall.
Bold is she
and wise as well.
Why waken me?
Go seek your guidance
from Erda's and Wotan's child!

WANDERER
You mean the Walküre,
Brünnhild, the maid?
She flouted the lord of the storm
    clouds,
when he had conquered the storm
    in his heart.
What the father of fights
had wished so warmly,
and what he forswore,
– against his own will –
this in her pride,
cold and contemptible,
Brünnhild dared to delight in,
Brünnhild, the wild warrior maid.
Wotan
pronounced her own doom,
when he sealed her eyes in sleep.
On the fell she slumbers fast.
She will awake,
the hallowed maid,
but to submit as bride to a
    man.
Could I seek counsel from her?

ERDA
Dazed am I,
since I awoke.
Wild and strange
spins the world.
My Brünnhilde,
the Wala's child,
suffers penance of sleep,
while her all-knowing mother
    slept?
Dare pride's teacher
punish pride?
Dare the deed's promoter
frown at the deed?
He who guards the law,

Tenderly, Erda reminds Wotan of
Brünnhilde, their child. The god's
conscience stirs: he delays his
answer with mere verbiage ('You
mean the Walküre, Brünnhild, the
maid?'). Who else could Erda
have meant?

Wotan's purpose in waking Erda
was to gain information. The out-
come is as unprofitable as their
earlier meeting in *Rheingold*.
Much to his surprise, Wotan
meets another Fricka in the earth-
goddess, whose moral arguments
are just as irrefutable.

(Wotan's Child)

der die Eide hütet,
wehret dem Recht?
herrscht durch Meineid?

Fate　*Oblivion*

Lass mich wieder hinab;
Schlaf verschliesse mein Wissen!

WANDERER
Dich Mutter lass ich nicht ziehn,
da des Zaubers mächtig ich bin.
Urwissend
stachest du einst
der Sorge Stachel

Erda

Götterdämmerung

in Wotans wagendes *Herz*;
mit Furcht vor *schmach*voll
feindlichem Ende
füllt' ihn dein Wissen,
dass Bangen band seinen Mut.

Wanderer

Bist du der Welt
weisestes Weib,
sage mir nun:

Treaty

wie *besiegt* die Sorge der Gott?

ERDA
Du bist – nicht

Ring

was du dich *nennst*!
Was kamst du störrischer
　　Wilder,

Liebe-Tragik

zu *stör*en der Wala Schlaf?

WANDERER
Du bist – nicht
was du dich wähnst!

Götterdämmerung

*Ur*mütter–Weisheit
geht zu Ende:
dein Wissen verweht
vor meinem Willen.

Erda

Weisst du, was Wotan – will?
Dir Unweisen

Götterdämmerung

ruf ich's ins *Ohr*,
dass sorglos ewig du nun schläfst.
Um der Götter Ende
grämt mich die Angst nicht,

Liebesnot

seit mein Wunsch es – *will*!
Was in des Zwiespalts wildem
　　Schmerze
verzweifelnd einst ich
　　beschloss,
froh und freudig

Bequest

führe frei ich nun *aus*:

who protects all contracts,
strikes at the law,
rules by misrule?
Let me vanish below;
sleep again seal my wisdom.

WANDERER
No, mother, you cannot leave,
for some potent magic is mine.
Wise Wala,
care's bitter barb
you once had planted
in Wotan's venturesome heart.
With fear of shameful,
fatal ending
you filled my senses,
and anguish bred in my breast.
Are you the world's
wisest of wise,
say to me now,
how the god may conquer his care.

ERDA
You are not
what you assume!
Why come here, headstrong and
    heedless,
to harrow the Wala's sleep?

WANDERER
You are not
what you would seem.
Wisdom of ages
lasts no longer.
Your knowledge must pale
before my purpose.
Hear then, what Wotan wills!
You unwise one,
listen to me,
and then forever sleep in peace.
The eternals' ending
cannot dismay me,
since I willed it so.
That which my own conflicting
    passions,
at war with themselves, once had
    planned,
proud and joyful
shall the god here ordain.

Wotan meets apathy wherever he turns. Both Fafner and Erda terminate their brief interviews by going to sleep, the one to possess, the other to dissociate herself.

The Bequest motif was originally intended for Wagner's Buddhist work *Die Sieger*, where it represented the central theme, joyful renunciation.

Motif	Text
	weiht ich in wütendem Ekel
Siegfried	des Niblungen Neid schon *die* Welt,
	dem wonnigsten Wälsung
Sword *Walhall*	weis ich mein Erbe *nun an.*
	Der von mir erkoren,
	doch nie mich gekannt,
	ein kühnster Knabe,
	bar meines Rates,
Ring + Sword	errang des Niblungen *Ring.*
	Liebesfroh,
	ledig des Neides,
	erlahmt an dem Edlen
Siegfried *Liebesnot*	Alberichs *Fluch*;
	denn fremd bleibt ihm die Furcht.
	Die du mir gebarst,
	Brünnhild
Bequest	weckt sich hold der *Held*;
	wachend wirkt
	dein wissendes Kind
	erlösende Weltentat.
Oblivion	Drum *schlaf* nun du,
	schliesse dein Auge;
	träumend erschau mein Ende!
	Was jene auch wirken –
Bequest	dem *ewig* Jungen
Liebesnot	weicht in Wonne der Gott.
	Hinab denn, Erda!
	Urmütter-Furcht!
	Ur-Sorge!
Oblivion	Hinab! hin*ab*!
Woodbird	zu ewgem Schlaf!

Though I bequeathed in my
    loathing
the world once to Alberich's quest,
the valiant Wälsung
shall now inherit the world.
He, my chosen champion
knows nothing of me.
The boy, bold and fearless,
free of my favour,
has won the Nibelung's ring.
Lavish in love,
free and unselfish,
this boy is not harmed
by Alberich's curse,
an alien ever to fear.
Your daughter and mine,
Brünnhild,
wakes to the hero's will.
Then your wisdom's
child shall achieve
a deed that redeems the world.
Go back to your sleep,
back to your slumber!
Dream and observe my downfall.
Whatever befalls now,
to youth eternal
yields the jubilant god.
Descend then, Erda!
Mother of care!
World-sorrow!
Away! Away
to endless sleep!
[Erda, with eyes closed, begins to
descend slowly. The storm has abated.
The moon lights up the scene.]

To the simultaneous proclamation
of the Sword and Walhall motifs,
Wotan comforts himself with soli-
loquizing, while telling Erda of
Siegfried's past, present and
future.

The confrontation between aged
god and ageless goddess ends
not with an exchange of insults,
but with the verdict that the age
of the gods is to give way to that
of mortals.

III. Akt: 2. Szene

Woodbird

WANDERER
Dort seh ich Siegfried nah'n.

Woodbird

SIEGFRIED
Mein Vöglein schwebte mir fort;
mit flatterndem Flug
und süssem Sang
wies es mich wonnig des Wegs:
Sword nun schwand es fern *mir da*von.
Am besten find ich
mir selbst nun den Berg;
wohin mein Führer mich wies,
Woodbird dahin wandr' ich *jetzt* fort.

WANDERER
Wohin, Knabe,
Woodbird heisst dich dein Weg?

SIEGFRIED
Woodbird Da redet's ja:
wohl rät das mir den Weg

Joy Einen *Fel*sen such ich,
von Feuer ist der umwabert:
dort schläft ein Weib,
das ich wecken will.

WANDERER
Wer sagt' es dir,
den Fels zu suchen,
wer nach der Frau dich zu sehnen?

Act III: Scene 2

[The Wanderer turns his face towards the centre of the stage.]

WANDERER
I see my Siegfried there.
[Siegfried's bird flutters ahead of him.
Suddenly it stops, as if alarmed, and flies
away.]

SIEGFRIED
The bird has flown from my sight.
With fluttering flight,
with sweetest song,
blithely it showed me the way;
but then it left me alone.
Now I must find me
the path to the fell.
The woodbird showed me the way,
and that way follow my feet.

WANDERER
My boy, tell me,
whither away?

SIEGFRIED [pauses and turns round]
What voice is this?
Perhaps it knows the way.
[he walks up to the Wanderer]
I would find a mountain
by fiery flames surrounded.
There sleeps a maid
who shall smile on me.

WANDERER
Who summoned you
to seek this mountain?
Who made you dream of the
    maiden?

Being chief god is a lonely business, and Wotan longs to communicate. Fricka repudiates him, Brünnhilde is banished, Mime is dead, Erda is laconic. That leaves Siegfried, the grandson, as a prospective interlocutor.

SIEGFRIED

Mich wies ein singend
Woodbird *Wald*vöglein:
das gab mir gute Kunde.

WANDERER

Ein Vöglein schwatzt wohl
    manches;
kein Mensch doch kann's verstehn:
wie mochtest du Sinn
Fafner dem Sang ent*neh*men?

SIEGFRIED

Das wirkte das Blut
eines wilden Wurms,
der mir vor Neidhöhl erblasste:
kaum netzt' es zündend
die Zunge mir,
da verstand ich der Vöglein
    Gestimm.

WANDERER

Erschlugst den Riesen du,
wer reizte dich,
den starken Wurm zu bestehn?

SIEGFRIED

Mich führte Mime,
ein falscher Zwerg;
das Fürchten wollt er mich
    lehren:
Sword *zum* Schwertstreich aber,
der ihn erstach,
Fafner *reiz*te der Wurm mich selbst;
seinen Rachen riss er mir auf.

WANDERER

Wer schuf das Schwert
so scharf und hart,
dass der stärkste Feind ihm fiel?

SIEGFRIED

Das schweisst' ich mir selbst,
Forge da's der Schmied nicht *konn*te;
schwertlos noch wär ich wohl
    sonst.

SIEGFRIED
There was a wondrous
woodland bird.
It sang those welcome tidings.

WANDERER
A bird will chirp and chatter

what no man understands;
so how could you tell
the song's true meaning?

SIEGFRIED
That came with a drop
of a dragon's blood,
whom I had killed at his cavern.
The burning blood
merely touched my tongue,
and then I could make sense of the
    song.

WANDERER
You fought an awesome foe.
Who urged you on
to slay the dragon, my boy?

SIEGFRIED
I followed Mime,
a fiendish dwarf,
who tried to teach me what
    fear is.
To deal the death-blow
that laid him low,
drove me the dragon himself,
with his juicy, jeering jaw.

WANDERER
Who forged the sword,
so sharp and keen,
that it slew so fierce a foe?

SIEGFRIED
I forged it myself,
since the smith was useless;
else I'd be still without sword.

A mare's nest of conflicting
impulses propels Wotan into this
fatal confrontation: he must test
Siegfried's fearlessness; he must
protect Brünnhilde; he must promote his own overthrow; he must
keep his oracular commitment
(*Walküre*, Act III) to prevent
access to the sleeping Brünnhilde.
His god-like fury is aroused by
Siegfried's taunts.

WANDERER
Doch wer schuf
die starken Stücken,
daraus das Schwert du dir
geschweisst?

SIEGFRIED
Was weiss ich davon!
Ich weiss allein,
dass die Stücken nichts mir nützten,
schuf ich das Schwert mir nicht
neu.

WANDERER

Wälsung Ordeal Das – mein ich wohl *auch*!

SIEGFRIED
Was lachst du mich aus?
Alter Frager,
hör einmal auf;
lass mich nicht länger mehr
Wälsung Ordeal *schwatz*en!
Kannst du den Weg
mir weisen, so rede:
vermagst du's nicht, so halte dein
Maul!

WANDERER
Geduld, du Knabe!
Dünk ich dich alt,
so sollst du Achtung mir bieten.

SIEGFRIED
Das wär nicht übel!
So lang ich lebe,
stand mir ein Alter
stets im Wege:
den hab ich nun fort gefegt.
Adventure *Stemmst* du dort länger
steif dich mir entgegen –
sieh dich vor, sag ich,
Woodbird dass du wie Mime nicht fährst!

Wie siehst du denn aus?
Was hast du gar
Wälsung Ordeal für 'nen grossen Hut?

WANDERER
But who made
the mighty pieces
from which you made the mighty
   sword?

SIEGFRIED
How should I know that?
I only know
that the pieces served no purpose;
therefore I forged them anew.

WANDERER [with a good-humoured
laugh]
Quite likely, my boy!

SIEGFRIED
Then why do you laugh,
ancient meddler?
No more delay!
Be off and keep me no longer!

Point me the way,
provided you know it,
but if you don't, then shut your big
   mouth!

WANDERER
Forbear, young fellow!
If I seem old,
you should respect me and fear me.

SIEGFRIED
Fear and respect you?
My whole life long
a doddering creature
was my keeper;
now he is out of the way.
Stand here no longer,
stubborn interferer.
On your way, fellow,
lest you should feel what he felt.
[he steps close up to the Wanderer]
You look very odd!
Why do you wear
such a monstrous hat?

Siegfried is as dauntless as he is
irreverent. Since Wotan created
him in his own image, the god
must not be surprised to find his
offspring true to his design.

Warum hängt dir der so ins
    Gesicht?

WANDERER

Wanderer

Das ist so Wandrers Weise,

Walhall   wenn dem Wind entgegen er *geht.*

SIEGFRIED

Walhall   Doch darunter fehlt dir ein Auge!
Das schlug dir einer
gewiss schon aus,
dem du so trotzig
den Weg vertratst?
Mach dich jetzt fort!
sonst möchtest du leicht

Walhall   das andre auch noch ver*lie*ren.

WANDERER

Walhall   Ich seh, mein Sohn,
wo du nichts weisst,
da weisst du dir leicht zu helfen.

Walhall   Mit dem *Au*ge,
das als andres mir fehlt,
erblickst du selber das eine,
das mir zum Sehen verblieb.

SIEGFRIED

Ha ha ha ha!
Zum Lachen bist du mir lustig!
Doch hör, nun schwatz ich nicht
    länger;
geschwind, zeig mir den Weg,
deines Weges ziehe dann du!
zu nichts andrem
acht ich dich nütz:
drum sprich, sonst spreng ich dich

Wotan's Frustration   fort!

WANDERER

Wotan's Frustration   Kenntest du mich,
kühner Spross,
den Schimpf – spartest du mir!
Dir so vertraut,
trifft mich schmerzlich dein

Wälsung Ordeal   *Dräu*en.
Liebt ich von je

Wotan's Frustration   deine *lich*te Art, –

Wherefore hangs it so over your
  eyes?

WANDERER
That is the way of wanderers,
when they walk against the wind.

SIEGFRIED
But one eye beneath it is missing.
Someone, I warrant,
has knocked it out,
when you so bravely
would bar his way.
Take yourself off,
or else you might lose
the only eye that is left you.

WANDERER
I see, my son,
all that you know
is how to be pert and unpleasant.
With an eye,
just like the one I have lost,
you look, my boy, at the other,
the one that's left for my sight.

It has often been suggested that
Wotan's lost eye represents the
sun, and/or that it had been
bequeathed to Siegfried. My suggested paraphrase reads: 'I had
given one eye to gain wisdom
[Prologue to *Götterdämmerung*].
This enabled me to create you.
You are my flesh and blood.'

SIEGFRIED
Ha ha ha ha!
A joke – that's all you are good for!
But hear, we chatter no longer.

At once, show me the way,
and your own way – find it yourself!
For you I have
no further use.
So speak, or savour my sword!

In his early *Der junge Siegfried*
Wagner omits the duel between
the Wanderer and Siegfried, who
is granted free passage to
Brünnhilde.

Wagner wrote to August Röckel
on 25 January 1857: 'There is once
more a stirring of his ancient
pride, brought about by his jeal-
ous concern for Brünnhilde. He
will not allow himself to be thrust
aside, but this is so little premed-
itated that in a sudden burst of
passion the longing for victory
overpowers him.'

WANDERER
If you but knew
who I am,
your scorn I would be spared.
Dear one to me,
I endure your defiance.

Long have I loved
your sterling stock,

(Wotan's Frustration)	Grauen auch zeugt' ihr
	mein zürnender Grimm:
	dem ich so hold bin,
	allzu hehrer,
	heut nicht wecke mir Neid,
	er vernichtete dich und mich!

SIEGFRIED

	Bleibst du mir stumm,
Wotan's Frustration	*stör*rischer Wicht?
	Weich von der Stelle!
	Denn dorthin, ich weiss,
Joy	führt es zur schlafenden *Frau*:
Woodbird	so wies es mein *Vög*lein,
	das hier erst flüchtig entfloh.

WANDERER

Grief	Es *floh* dir zu seinem Heil;
	den Herrn der Raben
	erriet es hier:
Treaty	weh ihm, holen sie's ein! –
Siegfried	*Den* Weg, den es zeigte,
Wotan's Frustration	sollst du nicht ziehn!

SIEGFRIED

Wotan's Frustration	Hoho! du Verbieter!
	Wer bist du denn,
	dass du mir wehren willst?

WANDERER

Wotan's Frustration	Fürchte des Felsens Hüter!
	Verschlossen hält
	meine Macht die schlafende Maid;
	wer sie erweckte,
	wer sie gewänne,
Wotan's Frustration	machtlos macht' er mich ewig! –
Loge	Ein Feuermeer
	umflutet die Frau,
	glühende Lohe
	umleckt den Fels;
	wer die Braut begehrt,
Magic Fire *Ride*	dem brennt entgegen die Brunst.

	Blick nach der Höh!
	Erlugst du das Licht?
	Es wächst der Schein,
	es schwillt die Glut;

though you will shake,
when my fury erupts.
You whom I love so,
you so lofty,
rouse my wrath not today.
It spells ruin for you and me.

SIEGFRIED
Still in my way,
stubborn old man?
Take to your heels now,
for this way, I know,
leads to the slumbering maid.
The woodbird had said so,
before it fluttered away.

WANDERER
It fled you to save its life:
it sensed the lord
of the ravens here;
peril follows its flight.
The way that it pointed,
you shall not go!

SIEGFRIED
Hoho! You forbidder!
Who is it then,
that dares to bar my way?

WANDERER
Bow to the fell's defender!
Confined I keep
by my might the slumbering maid.
He who would wake her,
he who would win her,
makes me mightless forever.
A sea of fire
encircles the maid.
Fervent those flames
that surround the rock.
He who craves the bride,
must boldly cross through the
    blaze.
Look up above,
and look at that light!
Its brightness spreads,
its brilliance grows.

In Mozart's *Die Zauberflöte*
Tamino seeks his beloved
princess, who is held captive; an
older man bars his way: 'Zurück!'
('Stand back!'). Tamino then
undertakes a perilous journey
through fire and water.

In *The Perfect Wagnerite* Shaw
writes: 'It is an excellent thing to
triumph in the victory of the new
order and the passing away of the
old; but if you happen to be part
of the old order yourself, you must
none the less fight for your life.'

	(Magic Fire)	sengende Wolken,
	Oblivion	*wa*bernde Lohe,
		wälzen sich brennend
		und prasselnd herab.
		Ein Licht-Meer
		umleuchtet dein Haupt:

bald frisst und zehrt dich
zündendes Feuer:–

Siegfried   zurück denn, ra*sendes* Kind!

SIEGFRIED

Joy   Zurück, du Prahler, mit *dir*!

Dort, wo die Brünste brennen,

Woodbird + Siegfried   *zu* Brünnhilde muss ich jetzt hin!

WANDERER

Siegfried   Fürchtest das Feuer du nicht,

Treaty   *Wotan's Frustration*   so sperre mein *Speer* dir den

Weg!

Noch hält meine Hand

der Herrschaft Haft;

das Schwert, das du schwingst,

Treaty   zerschlug einst dieser Schaft:

noch einmal denn

Wälsung Ordeal   zerspring es am ewgen *Speer*!

SIEGFRIED

Meines Vaters Feind!

Find ich dich hier?

Herrlich zur Rache

geriet mir das!

Sword   Schwing dei*nen* Speer:

Treaty   in Stücken spalt ihn mein Schwert!

Erda

WANDERER

Götterdämmerung   Zieh *hin*! ich kann dich nicht halten!

Liebe-Tragik

Wälsung Ordeal

Clouds are on fire,
as sweltering flames
will sweep in their fury
above and below.
A light-flood
will dazzle your sight,
[a fire on the summit grows brighter and
brighter]
and soon the blaze
will feast on your body.
Turn back, you hot-headed boy!

SIEGFRIED
Turn back, you braggart, yourself!
Fiery flames, let them blaze on;
to Brünnhilde now must I fly!

WANDERER [bars his way]
Have you no fear of the fire,
my spear then shall hinder your
  way.
My hand ever holds
that hallowed haft.
The sword that you swing,
once broke upon this shaft:
now once again
be splintered upon my spear!
[he stretches out his spear]

SIEGFRIED [draws his sword]
My own father's foe
here have I found!
Marvellous vengeance
is mine today!
Brandish your spear;
my sword shall shatter the shaft!
[With one blow Siegfried smashes the
Wanderer's spear. A flash of lightning
darts from it to the summit, where the
flames burn ever brighter. A clap of
thunder accompanies the blow. The
Wanderer quietly picks up the fragments of
his spear.]

WANDERER
Pass on! I cannot prevent you.
[he disappears in complete darkness]

The path to Brünnhilde is clear at
last. But at what cost! Fafner and
Mime had to be killed, and the
Wanderer humiliated and men-
tally destroyed.

SIEGFRIED

Mit zerfochtner Waffe
wich mir der Feige?

Joy · Ha, wonnige Glut!
Siegfried · Leuchtender *Glanz*!
Woodbird · *Strah*lend nun offen
steht mir die Strasse.–
Im Feuer mich baden!
Im Feuer zu finden die Braut!
Hoho! hahei!
Jetzt lock ich ein liebes Gesell!

Horn Call · Magic Fire · Horn Call
Siegfried · Horn Call · Siegfried
Joy · Woodbird · Horn Call
Siegfried · Loge · Horn Call
Oblivion · Sanctuary · Siegfried
Sanctuary · Siegfried · Joy
Woodbird · Joy · Woodbird
Oblivion · Fate

SIEGFRIED
With his broken spear
the braggart has vanished.
[the sea of flames begins to flare down the
mountainside]
Ha! Heavenly glow!
Glorious light!
Radiant, the road
runs open before me.
To bathe in that fire!
To find in the fire my bride!
Hoho! Hahei!
Come, consort, and answer my call!
[Siegfried plays his horn call and plunges
into the flames]

In three brief motifs (Joy,
Siegfried and Woodbird) the
Woodbird says 'Well done!' to
Siegfried.

For a discussion of the orchestral
transition between this scene and
the next, see overleaf.

Transition

This orchestral transition from scene 2 to scene 3 indicates that Siegfried's passage through the flames involves no fierce life-and-death struggle, but resembles a lover's buoyant journey to his beloved. The motifs tell the story to perfection: Horn Call – Magic Fire – Siegfried – Joy – Woodbird – Loge – Oblivion – Sanctuary – Fate.

Brünnhilde's Awakening (see also the Commentary on the Leitmotifs of Act III, p.164)

The four chords which signify Brünnhilde's revival are interspersed with harp arpeggios:

Transpose the melodic line of the four chords into the bass, and you have – the Dragon motif. Why? Brünnhilde as dragon? Ridiculous. Is it? The dragon as manifestation of human traits is a feature of sagas and fairy tales, where one meets maidens bewitched and transformed into serpents, who may be restored to their former selves by a spell-breaking kiss.

In *Walküre* (Act II), Brünnhilde appears to Siegmund, Siegfried's father. When the fated hero's noble demeanour arouses her sympathy, she declares, 'You must follow me now, for you have looked into my *consuming* eyes!' In the third act of *Siegfried* Brünnhilde's awakened passion for her awakener, Siegfried, makes her exclaim, 'When my eyes *feed* on yours, then are you not blind? Do you not dread this wild, love-driven maid?' Her voice is accompanied by cellos and double basses, intoning the Dragon motif.

What is Wagner's purpose in establishing a Brünnhilde/Dragon analogy? Freud and his disciples would see no problem here. Just as Siegfried can only satisfy the dragon's desire to consume him by plunging his sword into the monster, so Brünnhilde's desire to consume her lover can only be stilled by a similar act of penetration. It is not necessary to subscribe to this theory. Suffice it to state that Wagner – like Shakespeare before him and few after him – was familiar with the remotest recesses of the human heart, however complex, enigmatic or distressing. He was keenly aware of the interrelation of love and tragedy, of 'Liebe' and 'Tragik', his own life's motto and that of the *Ring*.

Sanctuary   Fate   Sanctuary
Freia   Fate   Sanctuary
Freia

III. Akt: 3. Szene

SIEGFRIED
Selige Oede
auf sonniger *Höh*!–

Joy   Woodbird Enchantment

Freia   Was ruht dort schlummernd

Ride   im schatti*gen* Tann?
Ein Ross ist's,

Wotan's Farewell   rastend in tiefem *Schlaf*!
Was strahlt mir dort entgegen?
Welch glänzendes Stahlgeschmeid?
Blendet mir noch
die Lohe den Blick?
Helle Waffen!
Heb ich sie auf?

Ha! in Waffen ein Mann:–
wie mahnt mich wonnig sein Bild!
Das hehre Haupt
drückt wohl der Helm?

Enchantment   *Leich*ter würd ihm,
löst' ich den Schmuck.

Enchantment   Ach! – wie schön! –
Schimmernde Wolken
säumen in Wellen
den hellen Himmelssee;
leuchtender Sonne
lachendes Bild
strahlt durch das
   Wogengewölk!

Act III: Scene 3

[Mountain summit, as at the end of *Walküre*. Morning mist. The fire is still blazing, further down the mountainside. Brünnhilde lies asleep, under a fir tree. She is in full armour, her helmet on her head, and her long shield covering her. Siegfried has reached the edge of the summit. He looks around in astonishment.]

SIEGFRIED
Blessed this haven
on sun-burnished heights.
What lies asleep
in the shade of a tree?
A war-horse,
resting in still repose.
What flashes flare upon me?
What glittering glints of steel!
Am I still blind
from the blaze of the flames?
Shining weapons!
Let me come close!
[he lifts the shield and sees Brünnhilde's form, but her face is largely covered by her helmet]
Ha! in armour, a man!
Remembrance stirs in my breast.
His noble brow
bruised by the helm?
Let him be freed
from his restraint.
[He removes the helmet. Long curls of hair trail down.]
Ah! how fair!
Shimmering cloudlets
fringe in fleeces
his glorious, lucid brow.
Sunlight's lustre,
laughing with joy,
burns through the billowy haze.

Violins and French horn play Wotan's Farewell motif. At this moment the god has truly parted from his child.

At the end of the first act of *Walküre* Siegmund presented Sieglinde with Nothung, his bridal gift. His son now wields the same sword to make Brünnhilde his bride.

Von schwellendem Atem
schwingt sich die Brust:–
brech ich die engende

Ride   Brün*ne*?
Komm, mein Schwert,

Sword   schneide das Eisen!

Enchantment   Das ist kein Mann!
Brennender Zauber
zückt mir das Herz;
feurige Angst
fasst meine Augen:
mir schwankt und schwindelt der

Wälsung Ordeal   Sinn!
Wen ruf ich zum Heil,
dass er mir helfe?
Mutter! Mutter!
Gedenke mein!

Wie weck ich die Maid,
dass sie ihr Auge mir öffne?
Das Auge mir öffne,
blende mich auch noch der Blick?

Wagt es mein Trotz?
Erträg ich das Licht?
Mir schwebt und schwankt

Wälsung Ordeal   und schwirrt es um*her*;
sehrendes Sehnen
zehrt meine Sinne:
am zagenden Herzen

Sanctuary   zittert die Hand!
Wie ist mir Feigem?

Wälsung Ordeal   Ist dies das Fürchten?
O Mutter! Mutter!
dein mutiges Kind!

Sanctuary   Im Schlafe liegt eine Frau:–
die hat ihn das Fürchten

Freia   ge*lehrt*!
Wie end ich die Furcht?
Wie fass ich Mut?
Dass ich selbst erwache,

Sword   muss die Maid ich erwecken!––
Süss erbebt mir

Liebesnot   *Enchantment*   ihr blühender Mund:

Such breezes, such breath,
such heart beat, such balm:
should I unharness the
 breastplate?
Come, my sword,
cut through the iron!
[He gently cuts the rings of mail and lifts off
the breastplate, revealing Brünnhilde
dressed in a female garment. He starts,
astonished and alarmed.]
This is no man!
Wondrous bewitchment
burns in my breast.
Anguish and awe
freeze me and blind me.
My senses falter – they fail.

On whom can I call?
Who will defend me?
Mother! Mother!
Be with me now!
[Almost unconscious, he sinks on
Brünnhilde's breast. Then he rises with
a sigh.]
How waken the maid,
To see her eyes look at my eyes?
Her eyes look at my eyes!
Will not their blaze strike me
 blind?
Dare I the deed?
Endure such a glow?
All sways and swirls,
all threatens and throbs.
Keenest longing
burns and consumes me.
O craven, my heart!
O coward, my hand!
Timorous fellow!
Is this what fear is?
O mother! mother!
Your child is alarmed.
A woman folded in sleep
has taught me the meaning of fear.

How conquer my fear?
How calm my heart?
So that I may waken,
must the maid be awakened.
Sweetly beckon
her blossoming lips.

In 1878 Herr and Frau Vogel sang
Siegfried and Brünnhilde in Munich.
Wagner sent him a telegram: 'If you
should find, in the third act, that
your wife has gone to sleep, please
wake her and give her my best
regards.'

Siegfried cuts through the rings of
mail 'on both sides', accompanied
by two clarinets in parallel thirds
– Wagner's ambiguous way of
illustrating the procedure, and/or
of commenting on the couple's
togetherness.

Having destroyed Fafner's heart,
Siegfried lays bare the heart of
Brünnhilde, which is to become
susceptible to human traits such
as imprudence and misjudgment.

What Siegfried would not learn
from Mime, he now experiences
at his first glimpse of a woman –
a psychological master-stroke.
None of Wagner's sources mentions this.

Wotan's kiss sent Brünnhilde to
sleep. Siegfried's kiss awakens
her.

wie mild erzitternd
mich Zagen er reizt!
Ach, dieses Atems
wonnig warmes Gedüft!
Erwache! erwache!

Fate heiliges *Weib*!
Sie hört mich nicht.
So saug ich mir Leben

Freia aus süssesten *Lip*pen –
Liebe-Tragik *sollt* ich auch sterbend vergehn!
Freia *Fate*
Freia **Revival**

BRÜNNHILDE

Revival Heil dir, Sonne!
Heil dir, Licht!
Heil dir, leuchtender Tag!

Fate *Lang* war mein Schlaf;
ich bin erwacht:

Siegfried *wer* ist der Held,
der mich erweckt?

SIEGFRIED
Durch das Feuer drang ich,
das den Fels umbrann;
ich erbrach dir den festen
  Helm:
Siegfried bin ich,
der dich erweckt!

BRÜNNHILDE
Heil euch, Götter!
Heil dir, Welt!
Heil dir, prangende Erde!
Zu End ist nun mein Schlaf;
erwacht seh ich:
Siegfried ist es,
der mich erweckt!

SIEGFRIED

Hosanna *O* Heil der Mutter,
die mich gebar;
Heil der Erde,
die mich genährt;
dass ich das Aug erschaut,
das jetzt mir Seligem lacht!

Their gentle quiver
has quenched all my dread.
Ah! but her breathing:
fervent, fragrant and fair!
Awaken! Awaken!
Maiden divine!
She hears me not.
New life I must drink
from those lips, those adored ones,
what though I die in a kiss!

Cosima quotes Wagner: 'The
lover's kiss is his first premonition
of death. That is why Siegfried is
so afraid.'

[He sinks, as if dying, on the sleeping
figure, and with closed eyes presses his
lips on hers. Brünnhilde opens her eyes.
Siegfried rises. She slowly raises herself
to a sitting position. Then, with a solemn
gesture, she greets heaven and earth.]

BRÜNNHILDE
Hail, my sunlight!
Hail, my sky!
Hail, my radiant day!
Long have I slept.
I am awake.
Who is the hero
wakened the maid?

The Edda contains the poem 'The
Lay of Sigrdrifa', in which Sigurth
wakes Sigrdrifa, who exclaims:
    'Hail to you, daylight!
    Hail to you, gods!
    Hail, earth, that gives us all!
    Who slit my breastplate?
    Who broke my sleep?'

SIEGFRIED
Through the flames I braved
that blaze around the fell.
Mine the hand that unloosed your
    helm.
Siegfried opened
Brünnhilde's eyes.

BRÜNNHILDE
Hail, Eternals!
Hail, fair world!
Hail, good earth in your glory!
My sleep is over now.
Awake am I.
Siegfried has
awakened the maid.

SIEGFRIED
I bless my mother,
giving me life;
bless this earth,
my fostering nurse.
Now I behold those eyes,
most blest am I of all men.

BRÜNNHILDE

Hosanna ⎤ O Heil der Mutter,
die dich gebar;
Heil der Erde,
die dich genährt;
nur dein Blick durfte mich schaun,
Siegfried **Jubilation** erwachen durft ich nur dir!
O Siegfried! Siegfried!
seliger Held!
Jubilation *Siegfried* Du *Wec*ker des Lebens,
siegendes Licht!
Hosanna O wüsstest du, Lust der Welt,

wie ich dich je geliebt!
Du warst mein Sinnen,
mein Sorgen du!
Dich Zarten nährt ich
noch eh du gezeugt,
noch eh du geboren
Bequest barg dich mein Schild:
so lang lieb ich dich, Siegfried!

SIEGFRIED

Wälsung Ordeal So starb *nicht* meine Mutter?
Jubilation Schlief die Minnige nur?

BRÜNNHILDE

Jubilation Du wonniges Kind,
deine Mutter kehrt dir nicht
Jubilation ⎤ wieder.
Du selbst bin ich,
wenn du mich Selige liebst.
Was du nicht weisst,
weiss ich für dich:
Bequest doch *wiss*end bin ich
nur – weil ich dich liebe.
Hosanna O *Sieg*fried! Siegfried!
Jubilation ⎤ siegendes *Licht*!
dich lieb ich immer;
denn mir allein
Death erdünkte Wotans Gedanke:
der Gedanke, den ich nie
nennen durfte;
den ich nicht dachte,
sondern nur fühlte;
Wotan's Child für den ich *focht*,
kämpfte und stritt;
für den ich trotzte
dem, der ihn dachte;

BRÜNNHILDE
I bless your mother,
giving you life;
bless this earth,
your fostering nurse.
My eyes are yours to behold;
and yours alone is my heart.
O Siegfried! Siegfried,
glorious youth!
You waker of life,
you conquering light!
Then hear me, you joy of the
  world,
ever beloved by me:
you were my courage,
my care were you.
Your life I fostered,
before you were formed.
Before you were born,
your shelter my shield.
All was love for you, Siegfried.

SIEGFRIED
My mother did not die then?
Was she merely asleep?

BRÜNNHILDE
You child of delight!
You will never know your own
  mother.
We are as one,
if I be blest with your love.
What you would know,
know it from me,
for wisdom comes to me,
because I love you.
O Siegfried! Siegfried,
conquering light!
I loved you ever,
for I divined
the root of Wotan's intention,
which I never dared to name
or to whisper.
I did not form it,
I only felt it.
For this I fought,
struggled and strove;
for this I flouted
him who had formed it;

The repeated rhythm of a dotted
quaver and two demisemiquavers
gives the Jubilation motif a par-
ticularly euphoric aspect.

Siegfried's question reveals the
tender, non-aggressive, non-
blustering side of his nature.

Brünnhilde's self-justification
does not necessarily prove Wotan
wrong in punishing her. Both
father and daughter acted according to their sincere convictions,
and both were right.

		für den ich büsste,
		Strafe mich band,
	Wotan's Child	weil ich ihn nicht *dach*te
		und nur empfand!
Bequest		Denn der Ge*danke* –
		dürftest du's lösen! –
	Hosanna	mir war er nur Liebe zu *dir*.

SIEGFRIED
Wie Wunder tönt
was wonnig du singst;

Hosanna   doch dunkel dünkt mich der *Sinn*.
Deines Auges Leuchten
seh ich licht;
deines Atems Wehen
fühl ich warm;

Hosanna   deiner *Stim*me Singen
hör ich süss;
doch was du singend mir sagst,

Fate   *Wälsung Ordeal*   staunend *ver*steh ich's *nicht*.
Nicht kann ich das Ferne
sinnig erfassen,

Hosanna   wenn alle *Sin*ne
dich nur sehen und fühlen.
Mit banger Furcht
fesselst du mich;
du Einzge hast
ihre Angst mich gelehrt.
Den du gebunden
in mächtigen Banden,

Liebe-Tragik   *Wotan's Frustration*   *birg* meinen Mut mir nicht mehr!
Ride   *Liebesnot*   *Ride*

BRÜNNHILDE
Ride   Dort seh ich Grane,
mein selig Ross:
wie weidet er munter,
der mit mir schlief!

Hosanna   Mit mir hat ihn Siegfried er*weckt*!

Jubilation   SIEGFRIED
Auf wonnigem Munde
weidet mein Auge:
in brünstigem Durst
doch brennen die Lippen,
dass der Augen Weide sich
labe!

for this I suffered
penance alone,
and his hidden secret
remained my own.
Wotan's intention –
can you not feel it? –
turned into love, love for you.

SIEGFRIED
How wondrous sounds
your winsome song,
yet dark its meaning to me.
I can see the splendour
of your eyes;
I can feel the fragrance
of your breath;
I can hear the sweetness
of your song;
but what you say in your song,
baffles my muddled mind.
Nor can I remember
days so far distant,
when now my own heart
hopes for nothing but your heart.
In bonds of fear
you have me bound.
You wonderful woman
have taught me to fear.
You who have bound me
with fear's mighty fetters,
give me my courage again!

BRÜNNHILDE
And there is Grane,
my sacred horse,
now gratefully grazing.
He slept by my side.
Now Siegfried has wakened us both.

SIEGFRIED
Your lips are my pastures,
fit for my feasting.
With feverish thirst
my own lips are flaming.
Where my eyes gaze, grant them
    their grazing.

BRÜNNHILDE
Dort seh ich den Schild,
der Helden schirmte;
dort seh ich den Helm,
der das Haupt mir barg:
er schirmt, er birgt mich nicht mehr!

SIEGFRIED
Eine selige Maid
versehrte mein Herz;
Wunden dem Haupte
schlug mir ein Weib:
ich kam ohne Schild und Helm.

BRÜNNHILDE
Ich sehe der Brünne
prangenden Stahl;
ein scharfes Schwert
schnitt sie entzwei;
von dem maidlichen Leibe
löst' es die Wehr:
ich bin ohne Schutz und
   Schirm
ohne Trutz ein trauriges Weib!

SIEGFRIED
Durch brennendes Feuer
fuhr ich zu dir;
nicht Brünne noch Panzer
barg meinen Leib:
nun brach die Lohe
mir in die Brust;
es braust mein Blut
in blühender Brunst;
ein zehrendes Feuer
ist mir entzündet:
die Glut, die Brünnhilds
Felsen umbrann,
die brennt mir nun in der Brust!
O Weib, jetzt lösche den Brand!
schweige die schäumende Wut!

BRÜNNHILDE
Kein Gott nahte mir je:
der Jungfrau neigten
scheu sich die Helden;
Walhall   *hei*lig schied sie aus Walhall!

BRÜNNHILDE
And there is the shield
that sheltered heroes;
and here is the helmet
that shielded my head;
they shield, they shelter no more!

SIEGFRIED
An all-conquering maid
has wounded my heart.
Wounds to my head
this woman has dealt.
I came without helm or shield.

BRÜNNHILDE
And there is my breast-plate's
shimmering steel;
a keen-edged sword
sundered its chain,
when the maiden's limbs
were stripped of their mail.
I am without sheltering
  shield,
without help, a hapless maid.

Brünnhilde realizes that loss of
godhead is tantamount to loss of
maidenhead.

SIEGFRIED
Through violent fire
I ventured to you.
No shield and no armour
sheltered my life;
but now those flames
do burn in my breast.
My blood is hot
with ardour of love.
A fire, a fire,
a passionate fire!
The blaze that burned
round Brünnhilde's rock,
now flames fiercely in my heart.
O maid, extinguish the blaze!
Stifle this feverish flame!
[he embraces her but, terrified, she
repulses him and flies to the other side]

BRÜNNHILDE
No god ever came close.
Before the maiden
bent low the heroes.
Chaste I parted from Walhall.

Siegfried

Wehe! Wehe!
Wehe der Schmach,
der schmählichen Not!
Verwundet hat mich,
der mich erweckt!
Er erbrach mir Brünne und
    Helm:
Brünnhilde bin ich nicht mehr!

SIEGFRIED

Bequest

Noch bist du mir
die träumende Maid:
Brünnhildes Schlaf
brach ich noch nicht.
Erwache! sei mir ein Weib!

BRÜNNHILDE

Mir schwirren die Sinne!
Mein Wissen schweigt:
soll mir die Weisheit schwinden?

SIEGFRIED

Bequest

Sangst du mir nicht,
dein Wissen sei
das Leuchten der Liebe zu mir?

BRÜNNHILDE

Curse

Trauriges Dunkel
trübt meinen Blick;
mein Auge dämmert,
mein Licht verlischt;
Nacht wird's um mich:
aus Nebel und Graun
windet sich wütend

Grief

ein *Angst*gewirr:
Schrecken schreitet

Liebesnot

und bäumt sich empor!

SIEGFRIED

Bequest

Nacht umbangt
gebundne *Augen*;
mit den Fesseln schwindet
das finstre Graun:
tauch aus dem Dunkel und
    sieh –
sonnenhell leuchtet der Tag!

BRÜNNHILDE

Wotan's Child

Sonnenhell
leuchtet der Tag meiner *Schmach*!

Deep my anguish;
deeper my shame,
my shame and disgrace.
He wounds my heart
who woke me to life.
He has broken breastplate and
    helm:
Brünnhilde am I no more!

SIEGFRIED
No, you are still
the slumbering maid.
Brünnhilde's sleep
is still her shield.
Awake, be a woman to me!

BRÜNNHILDE
My senses are reeling,
my reason sleeps.
Shall all my wisdom wither?

SIEGFRIED
Did you not sing,
your wisdom was
the light of your love for me?

BRÜNNHILDE
Trapped is in darkness,
troubled my sight.
My eyes are blinded,
the light is lost.
Night enfolds me.
Through murk and through mist,
tossing and trembling,
comes frenzy of fear.
Horror haunts me
and mounts to the sky.

SIEGFRIED
Night enshrouds
those eyes that are blindfold.
When the fetters fall,
then your dread will die.
Leap from the night and
behold:
    radiantly rises the day.

BRÜNNHILDE
Radiantly
rises the day of my shame.

Brünnhilde's changing emotions –
from rapturous welcome to shy
recoiling to total surrender –
remind us of her father's rapid
mood swings in the preceding
drama.

Idyll		O Siegfried! Siegfried!
		Sieh meine Anst!
		Ewig war ich,
		ewig bin ich,
		ewig in süss
		sehnender Wonne –
		doch ewig zu deinem Heil!
Liebesglück		*O* Siegfried! Herrlicher!
		Hort der Welt!
		Leben der Erde!
		Lachender Held!
		Lass, ach lass!
		lasse von mir!
		Nahe mir nicht
		mit der wütenden Nähe!
		Zwinge mich nicht
		mit dem brechenden Zwang!
		Zertrümmre die Traute dir
Liebesglück		nicht!
		Sahst due dein Bild
Idyll		im klaren *Bach*?
Sanctuary		Hat es dich Frohen erfreut?
		Rührtest zur Woge
		das Wasser du auf;
		zerflösse die klare
		Fläche des Bachs:
		dein Bild sähst du nicht mehr,
Jubilation		nur der Welle schwankend *Gewog*.
Liebesglück		So berühre mich nicht,
		trübe mich nicht:
Idyll	*Sanctuary*	*e*wig *licht*
		lachst du selig
		dann aus mir dir entgegen,
Jubilation	*Idyll*	froh und *heit*er, ein Held!
Sanctuary		O *Sieg*fried!
		leuchtender Spross!
Fate		*Lie*be – dich,
		und lasse von mir:
Sanctuary		vernichte dein *Ei*gen nicht!

SIEGFRIED
Dich – lieb ich,
o liebtest mich du!
Nicht hab ich mehr mich;
o hätte ich dich!
Ein herrlich Gewässer
wogt vor mir;
mit allen Sinnen
seh ich nur sie,

O Siegfried! Siegfried,
pity my fear!
Ever was I,
ever am I,
ever with fond,
feverish rapture,
and ever for your sweet sake.
O Siegfried! Glorious!
Wealth of the world!
Life of all being!
Hero sublime!
Leave, o leave!
Leave and forbear!
Do not come close
with your feverish frenzy.
Master me not
with your resolute might.
Destroy not your own heart's
 delight.
Seeing yourself
in the glassy brook,
does it not gladden your eyes?
Were you to trouble
the tranquil stream,
and shatter the shining
watery face,
yourself would you not see,
only ripples swirling around.
Therefore treasure the maid,
trouble her not!
Ever clear,
will your eyes then light
on me, your own likeness:
blithe, heroic and pure.
O Siegfried!
Child of delight!
Love yourself,
but let me be,
and do not destroy what is yours!

SIEGFRIED
I love you –
did you but love me!
Mine am I no more –
o were you but mine!
A fiery flood
before me rolls.
With all my senses
nothing I see

The sustained note and rising scale of the Idyll motif resembles the opening of the Quintet in *Meistersinger*. Both share the same emotion, blissful peace of mind.

To see one's reflection in water was one of Wagner's favourite poetic devices. Sieglinde: 'The brook has brought me my mirrored face'; Siegfried: 'In the crystal brook I saw myself.'

die wonnig wogende Welle:
brach sie mein Bild,
so brenn ich nun selbst,
sengende Glut
in der Flut zu kühlen;
ich selbst, wie ich bin,
spring in den Bach:

Sanctuary o dass seine *Wo*gen
mich selig verschlängen,
Bequest *Hosanna* mein Sehnen schwänd in der Flut!
Erwache, Brünnhilde!
Jubilation Wache, du *Maid*!
Lache und lebe,
süsseste Lust!
Sei mein! sei mein! sei mein!

BRÜNNHILDE
Jubilation O Siegfried! dein –
war ich von je!

SIEGFRIED
Warst du's von je,
Hosanna so sei es jetzt!

BRÜNNHILDE
Hosanna Dein werd ich
ewig sein!

SIEGFRIED
Was du sein wirst,
sei es mir heut!
Jubilation *Fasst* dich mein Arm,
umschling ich dich fest;
schlägt meine Brust
brünstig die deine;
zünden die Blicke,
Hosanna zehren die *Atem* sich;
Aug in Auge,
Mund an Mund:
Bequest *dann* bist du mir,
was bang du mir warst und wirst!
Jubilation *Dann* brach sich die brennende
Sorge,
ob jetzt Brünnhilde mein?

BRÜNNHILDE
Fate Ob *jetzt* ich dein?
Göttliche Ruhe
rast mir in Wogen:

but buoyant, sweet-surging billows.
Shattered my image,
mirrored no more –
scorched as I am,
I must cool in that torrent.
So now let me leap
into the flood.
O then, when the billows
so blissfully drown me,
then lulled were longing and love.
Awaken, Brünnhilde!
Waken, you maid!
Laughing and living,
dulcet delight.
Be mine! Be mine! Be mine!

BRÜNNHILDE
O Siegfried! Yours,
nothing but yours.

SIEGFRIED
Nothing but mine?
Then be it now!

BRÜNNHILDE
Yours shall I
always be.

SIEGFRIED
What you will be,
be it today!
Close in my arms
I clasp you to me.
Hot on my heart
your heart is beating.
My eyes are your eyes,
your breath is my breath.
Eyes on eyes
and lips on lips:
then you are to me
what always you were and will be.
Then stilled be the stifling
    anguish,
whether Brünnhild is mine.

BRÜNNHILDE
Brünnhilde yours?
Godlike forbearance
flares now in fury.

This paradox means that
Brünnhilde's former divine attrib-
utes, such as 'godlike forbearance' and 'virginal light' now give
way to human emotions which
'flare in fury' and 'blaze in
brilliance'.

keuschestes Licht
lodert in Gluten;
himmlisches Wissen
Hosanna stürmt mir da*hin*,
Jauchzen der Liebe
jagt es davon!
Fate Ob *jetzt* ich dein?
Siegfried! Siegfried!
Hosanna　　*Dragon* siehst due mich *nicht?*
Wie mein Blick dich verzehrt,
erblindest du nicht?
Wie mein Arm dich presst,
Hosanna entbrennst du mir *nicht?*
Wie in Strömen mein Blut
entgegen dir stürmt,
Ride *das* wilde Feuer
fühlst du es nicht?
Fürchtest du, Siegfried,
fürchtest du nicht
Siegfried *das* wild wütende Weib?

SIEGFRIED
Siegfried Ha!
Wie des Blutes
Ströme sich zünden,
wie der Blicke
Strahlen sich zehren;
wie die Arme
brünstig sich pressen;
Siegfried kehrt mir *zu*rück
mein kühner Mut,
und das Fürchten, ach!
das ich nie gelernt –
das Fürchten, das du
Woodbird mich kaum gelehrt:
das Fürchten – mich dünkt –
ich Dummer vergass es nun ganz!

BRÜNNHILDE
Valkyrie Cry　　*Ride* O *kindi*scher Held!
O herrlicher Knabe!
Du hehrster Taten
töriger Hort!
Jubilation *La*chend muss ich dich lieben;
lachend will ich erblinden;
lachend lass uns verderben –
Liebesbund lachend zu *Grunde* gehn!
Fahr hin, Walhalls
leuchtende Welt!

Virginal light
blazes in brilliance.
Heavenly wisdom
flies far away;
jubilant love
has hunted it hence.
Brünnhilde yours?
Siegfried! Siegfried,
can you not see?
When my eyes feed on yours,
then are you not blind?
When I clasp you close,
then do you not burn?
When my blood, like the sea,
storms surging at you,
its flaming fury
can you not feel?
Do you not fear
and do you not dread
this wild, love-driven maid?

SIEGFRIED
Ha!
As your blood will surge
against my blood,
as my eyes
will feed but on your eyes,
ever anchored
are your arms and my arms.
Now once again
I'm brave and bold,
and to fear, alas,
I have failed to learn.
This fear which your love
could scarcely teach,
this fear, I confess:
I fear I forgot how to fear.

BRÜNNHILDE
O hero-like child,
o child-like hero!
Of loftiest feats
the unwitting lord!
Laughing, so will I love you.
Laughing, let me be blinded.
Laughing, so let us perish;
laughing defy our doom.
Farewell, Walhall's
glittering world!

Brünnhilde's wish, 'Laughing let
me be blinded', points directly to
the next drama, where she proves
to be blind to Hagen's murderous
plot, and deaf to Waltraute's plea
to 'Ransom the gods from their
doom!'.

(Liebesbund) Zerfall in Staub
deine stolze Burg!
Leb wohl, prangende
Götterpracht!
End in Wonne,
du ewig Geschlecht!
Zerreisst, ihr Nornen,
das Runenseil!
Götterdämmerung,
dunkle herauf,
Nacht der Vernichtung,
neble herein!

Bequest *Mir* strahlt zur Stunde
Hosanna Siegfrieds Stern!
Liebesbund⌉ *Er* ist mir ewig,
ist mir immer,
Erb und Eigen,
Ein und All;
leuchtende Liebe,
Jubilation *Bequest* lachender *Tod*!

SIEGFRIED

Liebesbund⌉ Lachend erwachst
du Wonnige mir!
Brünnhilde lebt!
Brünnhilde lacht!
Hosanna⌉ Heil dem Tage,
der uns umleuchtet!
Heil der Sonne,
die uns bescheint!
Heil dem Licht,
das der Nacht enttaucht!
Heil der Welt,
da Brünnhilde lebt!
Sie wacht! sie lebt!
sie lacht mir entgegen!
Prangend strahlt
mir Brünnhildes Stern!
Liebesbund⌉ *Sie* ist mir ewig,
ist mir immer,
Erb und Eigen,
Hosanna *Ein und* All:
leuchtende Liebe,
Jubilation *Bequest* lachender *Tod*!
Siegfried *Jubilation* *Siegfried*

In dust may sink
its glorious walls.
Farewell, swaggering
pomp of gods!
End in bliss,
you eternal, great race!
You Norns must rend now
your rope of runes.
Dusk of gods
shall darken the day.
Night of their downfall,
dimly descend!
My life is ruled
by Siegfried's star.
He is for ever,
always mine,
my wealth, my world,
my one and all.
Living in love,
triumphant in death!

SIEGFRIED
Laughing you wake
in wonder to me.
Brünnhilde lives,
Brünnhilde laughs.
Blest the day
that blazes around us!
Blest the sun
that gives us this day!
Blest the light
that has burst from night!
Blest the world
where Brünnhilde lives!
Awake, she lives,
she smiles on her lover.
Proudly blazes
Brünnhilde's star.
She is for ever,
always mine,
my wealth, my world,
my one and all.
Living in love,
triumphant in death!

The curtain falls.

In writing off the gods and Walhall, Brünnhilde displays cosmic
recklessness. Siegfried showed
more human recklessness when
he awakened his bride: 'What
though I die in a kiss.'

Brünnhilde's invites the Norns to
rend their rope of runes – another
signpost to *Götterdämmerung*.

Wagner celebrates the brief,
ecstastic love union of Siegfried
and Brünnhilde in a perfect join-
ing of three motifs: Jubilation –
Bequest – Siegfried.

The final twelve bars are a joyous
affirmation of life and love,
authenticated by those constant
Woodbird trills in the woodwind.

Nothung, the Sword

As with other inanimate objects in the *Ring* (gold, Tarnhelm, treasure, ring and spear), the sword is present, seen or unseen, throughout the entire cycle. So before embarking on the final opera of the tetralogy, *Götterdämmerung*, it will be helpful to present the career of the sword 'Nothung'. Retracing its complex passage will serve as an ongoing aid to memory.

Few *Ring* motifs are endowed with such descriptive felicities as the Sword. Its opening interval of a rising fourth mirrors the action of a sword being withdrawn from its scabbard. The subsequent falling octave neatly depicts the sword's swooping exercise (be it splitting Mime's anvil or demolishing Wotan's spear). Finally, the music soars to its top note, celebrating the sword's achievement as it is brandished aloft.

The Sword motif first appears towards the end of *Rheingold*, accompanying Wotan's 'great thought'. He intends to create a free hero untainted by his own pragmatic dealings and malpractices, one who carries neither guilt nor responsibility. To him Wotan will bequeath a conquering sword to invalidate the law of cause and effect. At the *Ring*'s first performance, Wagner reportedly let Wotan, when gathering Alberich's treasure, pick up a sword that Fafner had left behind – a visual parallel to the Sword motif heard on the trumpet. He later dropped the idea, requiring the listener instead to recall the music of the Sword motif when, in *Walküre*, it is heard again, this time accompanying the appropriate action. A tall order.

In the first act of *Walküre*, as Sieglinde indicates to Siegmund the spot on the tree trunk where Wotan had plunged the sword, we hear the Sword motif, played first by bass trumpet, then by oboe and, for a third time, by cor anglais; the timbre of these instruments gives the motif a veiled, mysterious sound.

Later, at night, when Siegmund is alone in Hunding's hut, he recalls his father's pledge: 'A sword my father has promised, / to serve me in pressing need.' In the dim light of the hearth he at first fails to recognize the sword in the tree, preferring to see its golden shimmer as Sieglinde's 'radiant gaze', left there to linger behind. As he goes on to grip the sword-hilt, the Sword motif is heard on bass trumpet; as he pulls the sword from the trunk the motif is repeated, now in its original key of C major. Bass trumpet and four tubas proclaim the Sword motif which is heard again, in its original key, on trumpets and trombones.

The Sword motif, confidently pointed by the trumpets, begins the second act of *Walküre*. The act will end, however, with the sword shattered. Its first scene sets the confrontation between Wotan and his wife Fricka, who personifies the sanctity of wedlock. She demands Siegmund's death, 'Take back the sword / you gave to your son!' Wotan is unable to counter her argument and agrees to render the sword useless. He next encounters Brünnhilde, his and Erda's child, disclosing to her in despair that his grand design has come to nought. He has no choice. As law-giver and law-enforcer he will have to sacrifice his son.

Brünnhilde tries in vain to persuade her father to entrust her with Siegmund's protection in his forthcoming battle with Hunding, but only succeeds in drawing the god's impotent fury upon herself. To the falling octave, guillotine-like, of the Nothung motif, Wotan commands, 'Siegmund perish! / Such be the Walküre's work.'

Siegmund and Sieglinde escape from Hunding's house. With Nothung, as he calls his newly-won sword, Siegmund intends to kill his adversary. As trumpets mimic the sound of a splintered sword, Siegmund's exhausted sister-bride has a feverish premonition of his death and the splintering of the sword. Brünnhilde appears to Siegmund and to the simultaneous sounding of two motifs, Nothung and Fate, tells him of his impending doom. Siegmund learns that Wotan has invalidated the sword's power, and thwarted desire turns his remaining strength towards destroying both himself and Sieglinde.

This is more than Brünnhilde can allow. Flouting Wotan's command, she promises victory to Siegmund. The enemies meet. Brünnhilde stands by Siegmund, but Wotan shatters the sword and Siegmund falls. Brünnhilde seizes Sieglinde and, having gathered the splinters of the fickle sword, rides away with her. Brünnhilde secures Sieglinde's means of survival, and comforts her with the wonderful news that she will give birth to 'the greatest hero of all' – Siegfried. Only then does Brünnhilde defer to her father's judgement, hoping to mollify him with the news that Sieglinde has the splintered sword in safe keeping. But the wrathful Wotan punishes Brünnhilde by withdrawing her godhead and by locking her, asleep, on a rock surrounded by Loge's fire.

In *Siegfried* the young hero is at first unaware of the sword which awaits him. After his mother's death he was brought up by the smith Mime, who had obtained the splinters of Nothung but kept them hidden. Both Mime and his brother Alberich covet the ring and the golden treasure in Fafner's possession. (The giant has turned himself into a dragon and is sleeping on his hoard.) Mime plots Fafner's demise, intending Siegfried to kill the dragon with the sword forged from the splinters of Nothung. But Mime knows that reforging Nothung is beyond him, as what was bequeathed by a god and shattered by a god can be restored only by the god or a descendant of that god. The music makes this point by the simultaneous affirmation of the Sword and Walhall motifs.

Mime produces for Siegfried the splintered sword. At this point Wotan enters, disguised as a Wanderer, proposing a game of mutual questions and answers. The loser will lose his head. Mime cannot answer when asked by the Wanderer who is to forge the sword, and learns from his visitor that 'He who has never harboured fear, / he shall forge the sword. / Your cunning head, guard it with care. / I leave it forfeit to him / who has never harboured fear.' Mime knows only one person who is utterly fearless – Siegfried. The horns of the dwarf's dilemma dictate that he will lose his head to Siegfried unless the boy learns what fear is; but if he *does* learn fear, he will be unable to forge the sword which can kill the dragon.

Mime tries to teach Siegfried fear, but in vain, and the latter is more interested in reforging Nothung. So Mime hatches a plot to extricate himself from his predicament. While Siegfried works at the forge, Mime concocts a lethal drink which is to kill Siegfried *after* Fafner is slain.

At the end of the act Siegfried holds the newly forged Nothung aloft while Mime, no less exultantly, raises his noxious decanter. But Nothung's first task is one of peace: Siegfried cuts a reed to fashion a pipe and his blowing attracts the Woodbird. He then sounds his horn, waking the dragon. The stage direction at the end of the ensuing fight reads: 'Siegfried spies the position of the dragon's heart and plunges his sword up to the hilt.' The young hero dispatches the dragon to the accompaniment of the Sword motif which transforms itself into the Siegfried motif: master and sword are one. Nothung next slays Mime, whose evil plans the Woodbird had made known to Siegfried.

The third act of *Siegfried* provides two momentous meetings, first between Wotan and Erda, then between Wotan and Siegfried. To the simultaneous proclamation, *fortissimo*, of the Sword and Walhall motifs, Wotan soliloquizes, telling Erda of events past and present. He also informs her that he is resigned to relinquishing his tainted guardianship of the world, transferring it to his grandson, the unimplicated Siegfried. To test the boy's fearlessness, he bars Siegfried's path to Brünnhilde's rock, and has his own spear hacked from his hands by the intrepid young hero. Siegfried believes that his adversary is the man who had killed his father – which is, of course, not far from the truth.

After Siegfried crosses the circle of flames to find the slumbering Brünnhilde, Nothung's next task is one of love. It is used to cut through the rings of mail and release the sleeper: 'Come, my sword, /cut through the iron!'

In *Götterdämmerung* Brünnhilde bids her now beloved Siegfried to go forth to fresh adventures. He steps ashore at

King Gunther's hall, where he falls prey to the manipulations of Hagen, Alberich's son, whose magic potion makes him forget Brünnhilde and fall in love with Gutrune, Gunther's sister. Worse, he undertakes to help Gunther in his desire to marry Brünnhilde, and to that end they swear 'bloodbrotherhood'. Nothung serves to draw blood from Siegfried's arm, which he mingles with that of the ignoble Gunther.

Disguised through the power of the Tarnhelm as Gunther, Siegfried forces Brünnhilde to admit him to her bedchamber. Hagen's potion has made him forget that Brünnhilde is his own bride, but his innate virtue is still intact. He places Nothung between himself and Brünnhilde: 'To keep my pledge to my brother, / Nothung part me from his bride.' The act ends with forceful manifestations of the Nothung and Tarnhelm motifs, symbols confirming that Siegfried's real nature has been unwittingly and temporarily tarnished by events outside his control.

The real Gunther weds the betrayed Brünnhilde, and Siegfried allies himself to the worthless Gutrune. In a catastrophic confrontation between the former lovers, Brünnhilde denounces Siegfried. Both call upon Nothung to testify for them, but when the combined Sword and Treaty motifs are heard, a third motif, the murderous falling diminished fifth (the *diabolus in musica*) of Hagen, merges with the other two and devalues them.

In the last act of *Götterdämmerung*, when the Rhinemaidens warn Siegfried of his imminent death, the hero clings to his faith in the sword: 'The timeless rope of doom's decree, / even though curses cling to its cords, / Nothung shall slash it asunder!' Nothung had been programmed to do just that, to cut through the Norns' rope of destiny, to annihilate the chain reaction of cause and effect. Siegfried remains, to the end, Wotan's unwitting agent.

Hagen kills Siegfried. In the funeral music the trumpet's C-major Sword motif swells from *forte* to *fortissimo*, affirming the hero's integrity and the sword's endurance. Hagen's desperate attempt to wrest the ring from Siegfried's finger provokes a supernatural response. The dead man's hand raises itself against his murderer, the orchestral Sword motif adding its defiant comment.

Siegfried's and Nothung's innate integrity are celebrated at the end of the *Ring* when Brünnhilde, at last aware of the hero's innocence, proclaims:

No one so true,
so true to treaties
no one so pure.

The Sword motif sounds for a last time.

History of *Siegfried*

Composition History

1851	May	Prose sketch of *Der junge Siegfried* completed
1851	June	Prose draft of *Der junge Siegfried* completed
1851	June	Verse draft of *Der junge Siegfried* completed
1856	June	*Der junge Siegfried* renamed *Siegfried*
1856	September	Composition of *Siegfried* begun
1857	August	Composition of *Siegfried* discontinued
1869	March	Composition of *Siegfried* continued (Act III)
1871	February	Composition completed

Performance History

1876	August	First performance (as part of *Ring* cycle): Festspielhaus, Bayreuth
1882	May	First British performance: Her Majesty's, London

Bibliography

Further Reading

A more complete bibliography is given in the author's companion volume in this series.

Benvenga, N. *Kingdom on the Rhine* (Harwich, 1983)

Blyth, A. *Wagner's 'Ring'* (London, 1980)

Burbridge, P. & Sutton, R., eds. *The Wagner Companion* (London, 1979)

Cooke, D. *I Saw the World End* (London, 1979)

Coren, D. *A Study of Richard Wagner's 'Siegfried'* (diss., University of California) (Berkeley, 1971)

Coren, D. 'The Texts of Wagner's 'Der junge Siegfried' and 'Siegfried'' (*19th Century Music*, VI, 1982–3)

Dahlhaus, C. *Die Musikdramen Richard Wagners* (Velber, 1971; Eng. trans., 1979)

Donington, R. *Wagner's 'Ring' and its Symbols* (London, 1963)

English National Opera Guide: *Siegfried* (London, 1984)

Kobbé, G. *Wagner's Ring of the Nibelung* (New York, 1897)

Lee, M. O. *Wagner's 'Ring'* (New York, 1990)

Leroy, L. A. *Wagner's Music Drama of the Ring* (London, 1925)

McCreless, P. *Wagner's 'Siegfried'* (Ann Arbor, 1982)

Magee, E. *Richard Wagner and the Nibelungs* (Oxford, 1990)

Mander R. & Mitchenson, J. *The Wagner Compendium* (London, 1977)

Millington, B., ed. *The Wagner Compendium* (London, 1992)

Newman, E. *Wagner Nights* (London, 1949)

Osborne, C. *The Complete Operas of Richard Wagner* (London, 1990)

Porges, H. *Die Bühnenproben zu den Bayreuther Festspielen des Jahres 1876* (Bayreuth, 1881–96; Eng. trans., 1983, as *Wagner Rehearsing the Ring*)

Porter, A., trans. *Richard Wagner: The Ring* (London, 1976)

Shaw, G. B. *The Perfect Wagnerite* (London, 1898, 4/1923/repr. 1972)

Skelton, G. *Wagner at Bayreuth* (London, 1976)

Spencer, S., trans. *Wagner's Ring of the Nibelung* (London, 1993)

Spotts, F. *Bayreuth, A History of the Wagner Festival* (New Haven, 1994)

Weston, J. L. *The Legends of the Wagner Dramas* (London, 1896)

Discography

Four recommended performances. An extended discography can be found in the companion volume.

1956–8
Hans Knappertsbusch
Bayreuth Festival
Siegfried: W. Windgassen (1956, 1958), B. Aldenhoff (1957)
Mime: P. Kuen (1956, 1957), G. Stolze (1958)
Wanderer: H. Hotter
Alberich: G. Neidlinger (1956, 1957), F. Andersson (1958)
Fafner: A. van Mill (1956), J. Greindl (1957, 1958)
Erda: J. Madeira (1956), M. von Ilosvay (1957, 1958)
Brünnhilde: A. Varnay
These performances made the Bayreuth of the mid century a Mecca for connoisseurs and newcomers alike. Knappertsbusch's deep Wagnerian insight and Wieland Wagner's stunning production remain beacons undimmed. Windgassen's Siegfried, Hotter's Wotan, Neidlinger's Alberich and Varnay's Brünnhilde may have been equalled but never surpassed. My own preference is the 1958 version. Walhall on earth.
KING RECORDS KICC2274/88 (1956; Mono)
LAUDIS LCD15-4021 (1957, Mono)
ARCADIA HP48013 (1958; Mono)

1962
Georg Solti
Vienna Philharmonic Orchestra
Siegfried: W. Windgassen
Mime: G. Stolze
Wanderer: H. Hotter
Alberich: G. Neidlinger
Fafner: K. Böhme
Erda: M. Höffgen
Brünnhilde: B. Nilsson
In spite of its age, this studio-produced stereo set, digitally remastered, remains an exciting journey, with Solti revelling in the silken string tone, the ravishing woodwind and the climactic brass sonorities of the Vienna Philharmonic. Windgassen and Nilsson set the third act alight, and Joan Sutherland's Woodbird is an added, if unintelligible, bonus.
DECCA 414100-2DM15

1973
Reginald Goodall
English National Opera
Siegfried: A. Remedios
Mime: G. Dempsey
Wanderer: N. Bailey
Alberich: D. Hammond-Stroud
Fafner: C. Grant
Erda: A. Collins
Brünnhilde: R. Hunter
Goodall's spacious tempos reveal hidden treasures in Wagner's score, and allow his singers time to prepare their phrases with leisurely breath control. Rita Hunter's Brünnhilde, Alberto Remedios' Siegfried and Norman Bailey's Wanderer/Wotan are the inspired stars of this set which may well become a collector's prize.
EMI CMS763595-2 (sung in English)

1984
Marek Janowski
Dresden Staatskapelle
Siegfried: R. Kollo
Mime: P. Schreier
Wanderer: T. Adam
Alberich: S. Nimsgern
Fafner: M. Salminen
Erda: O. Wenkel
Brünnhilde: J. Altmeyer
As with Janowski's previous sets, the casting is inspired, and the orchestral sound ravishes the ear. Both Siegfried and the Wanderer (Kollo and Adam) are at the top of their careers, and to have such superb artists as Matti Salminen (Fafner), Siegmund Nimsgern (Alberich) and Peter Schreier (Mime) is a generous and much appreciated bonus. The digital recording is excellent.
EURODISC GD69006

Videography

There are four performances of *Siegfried* on video. The companion volume gives details of the other dramas of the cycle.

Place	Bayreuth	Munich	New York	Bayreuth
Orchestra	Festival	Bavarian. State	Met. Opera	Festival
Conductor	P. Boulez	W. Sawallisch	J. Levine	D. Barenboim
Producer	P. Chéreau	N. Lehnhoff	O. Schenk	H. Kupfer
Year	1980	1989	1990	1992
Video	Philips	EMI MVX9	DG 072	Teldec 4509
	070401/2/3/4	91275-3	418/19/20/21	91123-3
	3PHE2		3GH2	
Laserdisc	070 401-4	LDX9	072 418-21	4509
	1PHE2/3	91275-1	1GH2/3/3/3	91122/3-6 and
				94193/4-6

SIEGFRIED	M. Jung	R. Kollo	S. Jerusalem	S. Jerusalem
MIME	H. Zednik	H. Pampuch	H. Zednik	G. Clark
WANDERER	D. McIntyre	R. Hale	J. Morris	J. Tomlinson
ALBERICH	G. von Kannen	H. Becht	E. Wlaschiha	E. Wlaschiha
FAFNER	M. Salminen	P. Kang	F. Hübner	K. Moll
WOODBIRD	N. Sharp	J. Kaufmann	D. Upshaw	H. Leidland
ERDA	O. Wenkel	H. Schwarz	B. Svendén	B. Svendén
BRÜNNHILDE	G. Jones	H. Behrens	H. Behrens	A. Evans

Leitmotifs of *Siegfried*

In this alphabetical list of all leitmotifs in *Siegfried*, letters 'R' and 'W' are added when the motif appeared in *Das Rheingold* and/or *Die Walküre*.

Action

Adventure

Arrogance   R

Authority

Bequest

Brooding

Crisis   R, W

Crocodile

MIME

Als zul - len - des Kind zog ich dich auf,

Curse   R, W

Death   W

pp

pp

Dragon   R, W

Enchantment   R

Erda   R, W

Fafner

pp

Fate   W

Forge   R

Freedom

Aus dem Wald fort in die Welt ziehn: nim-mer kehr ich zu - ruck'

Freia

R, W

Genesis

R

Giants

R, W

Götterdämmerung

R

Grief

R, W

Horn Call

Hosanna

Idyll

Joy

R

Liebesbund

Liebesglück

(teurig, doch zart.)

O Sieg - fried, Herr - li - cher! Hort ____ der Welt!

Liebesnot   R, W

Liebe-Tragik   R, W

Loge   R, W

Longing

Magic Fire   W

Nibelungen Hate   R, W

Nothung   W

No - thung!

Oblivion   W

Revival

Rhinegold   R, W

Ride   W

Ring   R, W

Sanctuary   W

Shuffle

Siegfried   W

Sieglinde   W

Sword   R, W

Treasure   R

Treaty   R, W

Troth   R, W

Valkyrie Cry   W

Walhall   R, W

Wanderer

Wälsungen   W

Wälsung Ordeal   W

Woodbird

Wotan's Child

W

Wotan's Farewell

W

Wotan's Frustration

W

Photographic Acknowledgements

AKG London: 2
The Hulton Getty Picture Collection Ltd: 14
Mary Evans/Explorer: 98
Mary Evans/Arthur Rackham Collection: 17, 97
Mary Evans Picture Library: 18, 23, 94, 157, 158, 161, 162